AUTHORITY IN THE CHURCH:

A CHALLENGE FOR ANGLICANS

AUTHORITY IN THE CHURCH:
A CHALLENGE FOR ANGLICANS

by

G.R. Evans

with a Foreword by
The Most Revd H.R. McAdoo
Former Archbishop of Dublin

The Canterbury Press
Norwich

Copyright © G.R. Evans 1990

First published 1990 by The Canterbury Press Norwich
(a publishing imprint of Hymns Ancient & Modern Limited)
St Mary's Works, St Mary's Plain,
Norwich, Norfolk, NR3 3BH

British Library Cataloguing in Publication Data
Evans, G.R. (Gillian Rosemary) *1944* -
Authority in the church.
1. Church of England. Authority
I. Title
262.8

ISBN 1-85311-017-5

*Typeset by Gingivere of Cambridge
and printed in Great Britain by
St Edmundsbury Press Limited
Bury St Edmunds, Suffolk*

Contents

Foreword

This is a book which compels the reader to get the contemporary inter-Church scene into focus and perspective. It is written from within the context of 'the universal Church sharing catholicity even in broken or impaired communion' (p. 6). The author is deeply conscious of the value of the Anglican identity in itself and as an enrichment of a united Church. Dr. Evans analyses the complex implications of provincial autonomy and of the ordination of women within the framework of a widely-researched and fascinatingly documented study of authority in the Church: in Scripture, in Order, in the local community, in faith and in morals. She has a vision of Anglicans going forward with fellow-Christians into the extended unity of catholicity in a future united Church.

Throughout the centuries down to our own time the area of authority has been one in which controversy and problems have continued to abound. This book leads the reader through past and present difficulties towards a search for a common faith and order. The chapter on the ecclesiology of the ordination of women raises acute problems in respect of concepts of ministry and of provincial independence and interdependence, 'but it can be made, under providence, into an opportunity to make great strides ecumenically' (p. 82). Dr. Evans's appeal for patience in charity is moving and compelling. But have we, in all this, as still divided and separated Churches, taken cognisance of the uncomfortable New Testament concept of the *kairos*, the possible time of opportunity or fulfilment? To allow for the unprecedented situation or the creatively confrontational emergency is not *necessarily* to construct a post-dated alibi but to recognize that this has been a recurring element, sometimes even a prophetic value, in the course of the Church's mission in time and space. Such considerations have to be set firmly over against the call to maintain universality in a divided Church.

The way in which Anglicans have approached this through the Reformation period and ever since is to assert, with Jewel, that their Church is no new Church with no new dogmatic system. Laud, Bramhall and Beveridge spoke for a Church when they simply identified themselves as 'catholic Christians' (pp. 5-6). Archbishop Benson of Canterbury speaking in Ireland in 1896 put it thus: 'our Church created no new fictitious platform of authority. It was, and it relied upon itself as, the ancient Catholic Church.' Anglicans hold this to be historically and theologically demonstrated through the appeal to Scripture, to tradition and to reason. This, together with the distinction between fundamentals and secondary matters, has been an essential element in the Anglican ethos. It is because of, and indeed by means of, this assertion of an undifferentiated Catholicism that no contradiction is felt in being robustly Anglican and robustly ecumenical at the same time. For the identity of Anglicanism is not dependent on or involved with the assertion of particular dogmas or theological systems seen as essentially characteristic of its affirmation of 'the faith once for all delivered'. A comment by the present Archbishop of York bears directly on all this: 'Only Catholic tradition is rich enough and stable enough to be able to offer something distinctive to the world without being captured by the world. But it must be a Catholicism which is true to its highest vision, and hence broad enough, hospitable enough, rooted sufficiently in sacramental reality, confident enough in its inheritance to be able to do new things, diverse enough, and yet passionately enough concerned about unity, to be genuinely universal. At the moment neither Roman Catholicism nor Anglo-Catholicism measure up to this standard'.

While the three-fold appeal is not exclusive to Anglicanism it can fairly be claimed that no other Church in its formularies and in the writings of its theologians past and present has so consistently and explicitly made this appeal the criterion for maintaining the Church in the truth of the Gospel - the primary objective of authority in the Church.

How fares this element in the Anglican identity today? In the contemporary scene two forces are detectable which ultimately would appear to be hostile to what Lambeth 1948 termed this 'dispersed' and 'organic' authority which 'possesses a suppleness and elasticity in that the emphasis of one element over the others may and does change with the changing conditions of the Church' (*Report*, p. 85). These forces are Scriptural fundamentalism, the more or less literalist view of that which is normative for authority in the Church, and a fundamentalism of tradition seen in terms of a fly-in-amber rather than as the living Church interpreting the faith 'once for all delivered' in the idiom and life-setting of each generation. Both impair the suppleness of a dispersed authority and the confidence of a Catholicism able to face the challenge of changing perceptions of what is right for 'the members of God's household who are being built together to become a dwelling in which God lives by his Spirit' (Eph. 2.21-22).

Archbishop Michael Ramsey observed in 1960 that 'the times call urgently for the Anglican witness to Scripture, tradition and reason - alike for meeting the problems which Biblical theology is creating, for serving the reintegration of the Church, and for presenting the faith as at once supernatural and related to contemporary man' (*From Gore to Temple*, p. ix). Have the developments of the intervening three decades impaired the effectiveness of this distinctive method of maintaining the Church in the truth? Only, I would suggest, if we persist in viewing the three-fold appeal through seventeenth-century or nineteenth-century spectacles. Something like this intuition is suggested by Peter Coleman in a recent number of

Theology: 'It is commonly said that the Anglicans base their perception of Christian truth on Scripture, Tradition and Reason. But this three-fold dialectic is beginning to look like a methodological strait-jacket for a Church which no longer actually lives inside it. There are at least four components which need reconciling in the Anglican Communion at the moment. Tradition actually means that point in development now reached by the Western Catholic Church. This tradition can change abruptly, as with its vernacular liturgy, so it is not necessarily preservative. Scripture means careful attention to the biblical texts, with exegesis and hermeneutics taken seriously, and is by no means confined to fundamentalism. Reason among Anglicans no longer means building the kind of logical structure of doctrine and ethics from certain clear bases that was still possible, say, in the days of Bicknell's *Thirty-Nine Articles* (1919). It means estimating continually the God-given value of experience, and not merely following the spirit of the age. The fourth component, which is more difficult to label than describe, is spontaneity ... the freedom of God's people to be spontaneous in what they sense ought to be done now is a permanent element of the Christian tradition'.

Developments in all three areas there have been but many would hold that these have ultimately been beneficial to the operation of the appeal. They would claim to see a more integrated view of Scripture, a return to the earlier concept of tradition as the living Church interpreting the faith consonantly with Scripture, and an altogether richer understanding of the nature and role of reason in religion.

Not that this assessment is all that new - did not Jeremy Taylor (1613-1667) write that 'Scripture, tradition, councils and Fathers, are the evidence in a question, but reason is the judge'. Had he not just such a sensitive appreciation and understanding of reason when he wrote that it is 'a transcendent that runs through all topics' and insisted that 'our reason does not consist in a mathematical point: and the heart of reason, that vital and most sensible part, is an ambulatory essence, and not fixed'.

In the measure in which it is true to its own best self - understanding Anglicanism makes its best contribution to the unity of Christians. It may well be that further investigation is needed of reception in a universal Church suffering impaired communion and in a local Church going through the process of reception. Perhaps too, there is a need to arrive at some consensus and understanding about dissent - a matter raised also at the 1974 Synod of Bishops in Rome.

Here is a book which will inform and enlighten those facing this complex of questions concerning the nature and function of authority in the Church.

March, 1990 + *H.R. McAdoo*

Preface

At the Lambeth Conference of 1988, on August 1st, the Conference passed a Resolution after a day of troubled debate. The intention was to limit as far as possible the damage which would be done to communion between the Anglican provinces if one province consecrated a woman bishop while others were not yet able to accept that a woman could hold episcopal office. The resulting impaired communion, it was clearly seen, would come about not as a consequence of mere 'disapproval' of such an action, but automatically. It would become impossible for priests ordained by a bishop not all Anglicans could recognise, to be themselves recognised as priests everywhere in the Anglican Communion. There would be an internal problem of mutual recognition of ministry to add to those which already exist between separated Churches throughout the world.

The Resolution spoke of mutual respect and courtesy, the importance of maintaining 'the highest possible degree of communion with Provinces which differ'. It wanted to see 'continuing consultation with other Churches as well as examination of the relationship between churches of the Anglican Communion', of the need for 'open dialogue' and 'consultation' and the making of 'pastoral provision'.[1] It did the best that could be done in the circumstances. But the Conference was struggling with a problem which has beset Christianity from the first missionary days, that of discovering and maintaining the right balance between the universal and the local in the Church founded by Jesus Christ.[2] It was apparent that the questions which were arising cannot ultimately be resolved except in ecumenical terms. And indeed, on the following day, a long series of ecumenical Resolutions was warmly and almost unanimously welcomed.

This study tries to provide a working brief on the inter-relationship of the complex of 'authority' questions which confronts the Anglican Communion today, most noticeably in this area of 'provincial autonomy', but on many other fronts too; and to do so in the context of a goal of universality. Much might be said on the modern debate, but that would take a far longer book, and I have simply kept here to the main lines of the classic issues.

---

1   The text of the Resolution is published in *The Truth Shall Make You Free*, Resolution and Reports of the 1988 Lambeth Conference, SPCK (London, 1988), p. 201.

2   E. Dvornik, 'National Churches and the Church Universal', *Eastern Churches Quarterly* 5 (1943), pp. 172-218.

Acknowledgements

I should like to thank the British Academy, whose grant of a Research Readership (1986-8) made possible research for this study, as well as other work; the members of the Faith and Order Advisory Group of the Church of England's Board for Mission and Unity, and the Archbishops' Group on the Episcopate, for comments and suggestions at the stage when I was drafting parts of this study as background papers for the work of these bodies. I have to thank the Chairmen of these Groups for their willingness to allow portions of these texts ultimately adopted by the Groups also to stand as pages of this book. Others have helped in many ways by their response to questions and their willingness to read parts of the text. I am especially grateful to The Most Revd H.R. McAdoo, The Revd Professor Sir Henry Chadwick, The Revd John Halliburton, The Revd Michael Jackson, Robert Ombres O.P., The Right Revd Stephen Sykes.

Abbreviations

(Ecumenical dialogues are to be found in *Growth* unless full details are given here)

Acta CT	Acta Concilium Tridentinum.
A-L	Anglican-Lutheran Dialogues.
Ambrose	Ambrose, *De Officiis Ministrorum,* in CSEL.
The Anglican Homilies	The Anglican Homilies (London, 1833 edition, reprinted London, 1986).
A-O	Anglican-Orthodox Dialogues.
Apo	John Henry Newman, *Apologia pro vita sua* (ed. of 1865).
Aquinas ST	Aquinas, *Summa Theologiae*, in the edition of Rome (1882 ff.).
A-R	*God's Reign and our Unity:* Report of the Anglican-Reformed International Commission (1984).
Ball	T.I. Ball, *The Orthodox Doctrine of the Church of England* (London, 1877).
Bramhall, *Vindication*	John Bramhall, *A Just Vindication of the Church of England, Works*, Vol. 1 (Oxford, 1842).
Beveridge, *Ecclesia Anglicana*	William Beveridge, *Ecclesia Anglicana, Ecclesia Catholica, Works*, Vol. 11 (Oxford, 1840).
Bicknell	E.J. Bicknell, *A Theological Introduction to the Thirty-Nine Articles* (London, 1919, third ed., 1955).
Booty	in Sykes, qv.
B-R	Baptist-Reformed Dialogues.

Calvin, *Institutes*

Calvin, *Institutes* in CR and several modern editions.

Canon

The Canons of the Church of England (London, 1969).

Cardwell, *Synodalia*

Synodalia, ed. E. Cardwell, 2 vols. (1842, repr. 1966).

Care

Henry Care, *The Nine and Thirty Articles* (1682).

Cary

Henry Cary, *Testimonies of the Fathers of the first four centuries to the doctrine and discipline of the Church of England* (1835).

CCSL

Corpus Christianorum Series Latina.

Christian Authority

Christian Authority: Essays Presented to Henry Chadwick, ed. G.R. Evans (Oxford, 1988).

Church and State

Church and State, Report of the Archbishops' Commission (1970, Church of England).

Codex Iuris Canonici

Codex Iuris Canonici (Vatican, text of 1983).

Coverdale, *Remains*

Coverdale, *Remains* PS (1846).

C R

Corpus Reformatorum.

CSEL

Corpus Scriptorum Ecclesiasticorum Latinorum.

Cranmer, *Remains*

Cranmer, *Remains* PS (1833).

Deacons in the Ministry

Deacons in the Ministry of the Church (Report of 1987, Church of England).

Didache

Didache, ed. J.B. Lightfoot, *The Apostolic Fathers* (1891).

Doctrine Commission

Doctrine Commission, 1922 *Report* (London, 1938).

Emmaeus

The Emmaeus Report, Anglican Consultative Council (1987).

Gerson, *De Concilio Generali*	Jean Gerson, ed. L. Dupin (Amsterdam, 1706), in *Opera Omnia*.
Gibson	E. Gibson, *Synodus Anglicana*, ed. E. Cardwell (1854).
Goode	W. Goode, *Tract XC Historically Refuted* (London, 1854, second ed., 1866) and *Holy Scripture the Sole Authoritative Exposition of the Faith* (London, 1862).
Gregory the Great	Gregory the Great, *Regula Pastoralis*, in CCSL.
Growth	*Growth in Agreement*, ed. H. Meyer and L. Vischer (Geneva, 1984).
Gundrum	J.R. Gundrum, *The General Convention*, Arrington Lectures, University of the South, 1982.
Hammond	Henry Hammond, *Of Fundamentals* and *Of the Reasonableness of Christian Belief*, *Works* (Oxford, 1849), Vol. 2.
Hickes	George Hickes, *The Dignity of the Episcopal Order*, *Works* (Oxford, 1847), Vol. 2.
Hooker, *Laws*	Richard Hooker, *The Laws of Ecclesiastical Polity*, ed. R.W. Church and F. Paget (Oxford, 1888).
Hooker, *A Christian Letter*	Hooker, *A Christian Letter* (1599), ed. J.E. Booty (Cambridge, Mass., 1982).
Keble	Keble, *Sermons for Saints' Days and Holy Days* (Oxford, 1875-).
Kidd	J.B. Kidd, *The Appeal to Antiquity as a Principle of the English Reformation* (Oxford, 1901).
Kidd, Richard Bentley Porson	Richard Bentley Porson Kidd, *Testimonies and Authorities* (1848).
Lambeth	Lambeth Conference Resolutions and Reports quoted from *Five Lambeth Conferences* (London, 1920), for 1867-

	1908; *The Lambeth Conferences* (London, 1948), for 1920, 1930 and 1948; and from the separate *Reports* for 1958, 1968, 1978 and 1988.
Lathbury	T. Lathbury, *A History of the Convocation of the Church of England* (London, 1853).
Laud, *Fisher*	William Laud, *Conference with Fisher*, ed. W. Scott, *Works* (Oxford, 1849), Vol. II.
Luther	Works cited from Weimar Ausgabe.
Miller	Joseph Miller, *The Thirty-Nine Articles of the Church of England* (1878).
The Nature of Christian Belief	Statement of the House of Bishops (London, 1986).
Newland	T. Newland, *An Analysis of Bishop Burnet's Exposition of the Thirty-Nine Articles* (Dublin, 1829).
Niagara	*The Niagara Report* of the International Anglican-Lutheran Commission (1987).
Owen, *Of Schism*	John Owen, *Of Schism, Works*, ed. W.H. Goold (1850, repr. London, 1967), Vol. 13.
PL	*Patrologia Latina.*
PS	Parker Society. The sixteenth century Anglican divines are cited from this series.
Peter Lombard, *Sentences*	Peter Lombard, *Sentences* (Quarracchi, 1971- ff.).
Resp.	*Towards a Church of England Response to BEM and ARCIC* (CIO, London, 1985).
Suenens, *Coresponsibility*	Cardinal Suenens, *Coresponsibility in the Church* (London, 1968).
Suenens, *Dossier*	Cardinal Suenens, *Dossier*, ed. J. de Broucker (1970).

Sykes	*Authority in the Anglican Communion*, ed. S. Sykes (Toronto, 1987).
Taylor, Episcopacy Asserted	Jeremy Taylor, Episcopacy Asserted, *Works*, ed. C.P. Eden (London, 1847-54) Vol. V.
Thorndike	H. Thorndike, *Of the Principles of Christian Truth, Works* (Oxford, 1845) Vol. II.
Tracts for the Times	Tracts for the Times (London, 1834-41).
Tyrrell Green	E. Tyrrell Green, *The Thirty-Nine Articles and the Age of the Reformation* (1896).
Vatican II	*Conciliorum Oecumenicorum Decreta*, ed. J. Alberigo *et al.* (3rd ed., Bologna, 1973).
Veneer	J. Veneer, *An Exposition of the Thirty-Nine Articles of the Church of England* (London, 1730).
Waterland	Daniel Waterland, *A Discourse of Fundamentals, Works* (Oxford, 1856), Vol. 6, and *Remarks upon Dr. Clarke's Exposition of the Church Catechism*, Vol. 4.
Whitgift, Cartwright	Whitgift on the debate about Cartwright's *Epistle to the Church of England*, PS.

Chapter One

Introduction

What does it mean to speak of 'a Church'? There is much less difficulty in defining 'the Church' or 'a church'. When we speak of 'a church' we usually mean a local worshipping congregation. We use 'the Church' for the mysterious 'body of Christ', which includes all Christians everywhere in all the ages. But talk of 'a Church' can imply division, the existence of an ecclesial body which identifies itself in such a way that the believer may come to speak of himself first as a member of such a body rather than as 'a Christian'. 'I am an Anglican'; 'I am a Methodist'; 'I am a Lutheran', and so on.

That should bring us up short.

Some Anglican scholars have recently been suggesting that the 'integrity' of a Church depends on its being true to what it understands to be its 'identity'.[1] 'There is no such thing', argues one, 'as undifferentiated Christianity'.[2] But others would say that 'there is no separate Anglican identity',[3] for Anglicans must first of all call themselves Christians.

We must begin with this controversy, because much hangs upon it. The first thing to be said is that those things which are dear and familiar in the life of a beloved Church are not at issue. It is always the case, and rightly so, that the experience of common life and worship in one's own Church has a distinctive style and flavour. It reflects the uniqueness of the persons who make up the body of Christ in every place. Nor is there any problem about the existence of regional or national Churches. There has always been a perfectly proper local loyalty in Christianity. That is one of the factors which bind people at a human level in the fellowship of communion (*koinonia*). Paul wrote his letters to the Churches in recognition of that. The difficulty arises when a Church thinks of itself as holding a distinctive faith which makes it different from other communities of Christians.

All this is of the first importance ecumenically, for two reasons. First, the method ecumenical conversations use to arrive at a common statement is

---

[1] S. Sykes, *The Integrity of Anglicanism* (Mowbray, London and Oxford, 1978), p. 4.
[2] Paul Avis, *Anglicanism and the Christian Church* (T. and T. Clark, Edinburgh, 1989), p. 6.
[3] John Howe, *Highways and Hedges: Anglicans and the Universal Church* (London, 1985), p. 28.

bound to be partly determined by the view the participants take of their ecclesial 'identity'. If, as Paul Avis suggests, 'each side needs to know what the other stands for' and 'what it itself stands for' (p. 6), it is hard to see how an adversarial stance is to be avoided, and some element of trading and bargaining and even compromise with it. In the experience of those who have been engaged in ecumenical dialogues, that is not what happens. Again and again members representing one Church find themselves putting forward arguments traditionally deemed the property of the other, as all become more and more deeply committed to what becomes a common quest. The search for the truth comes to be all-important, and it is seen as one truth to be owned by all Christians. There is no question of either side having to give up anything precious within its tradition. What is achieved is gain for both sides. That brings us to the second reason: on Avis's assumption, the ecumenical end in view must put high on the agenda the preservation of a denominational ecclesial 'identity'. That raises large questions about the character of unity in a future united Church.

The ecclesial identity of the local Church is both an ancient and a right identity, but it is not to be seen as simply that of a part within the whole. It is rather, as Ignatius the first bishop of Antioch - and the Orthodox tradition[4] - stress, that of a whole within the whole, a mystery in which the local Church, the 'Church in each place', is fully the Church, because it is also in microcosm the universal Church.

I have argued in this study that only when Christians so 'identify' themselves can they be truly free to enjoy the diversity of style and character of life and worship together which reflects local needs and local inheritance.

Structurally speaking, local Churches must, of course, behave as parts of a whole. That has been the pattern in episcopal Churches, and is increasingly so in non-episcopal Churches as they evolve structures of supra-congregational oversight. But here again the local and particular Church stands committed by the bonds of love to act in charity and with patience towards other Churches, and this, too, is a main theme of what follows.

Anglicans share a common historical and geographical origin as a separate Communion. They have a 'constitution' which can be found in a whole range of history, precedent, legislation and literature.[5] Yet 'English' is not now, and has long not been, a synonym for 'Anglican'. There is still, in its essentials, a common liturgy, but no longer a single Prayer Book; indigenous liturgies have been replacing the Elizabethan text since the

---

[4]   AO, 13.
[5]   Lambeth, 1978, pp. 98-9.

seventeenth century (when the Scottish Episcopal Church produced its own Prayer Book). Anglicans no longer share a fully interchangeable ministry because some provinces have moved ahead of others in the ordination of women, and not all parts of the Communion have as yet been able to accept their ministry.

William Laud (1573-1645), one of the seventeenth century Archbishops of Canterbury, thought that 'The Roman Church and the Church of England are but two distinct members of that Catholic Church which is spread over the face of the earth ... Rome and other ... Churches are in this universal catholic house as so many daughters, to whom, under Christ, the care of the household is committed by God the Father, and the Catholic Church, the mother of all Christians'.[6] It is still important today to see the internal strains and tensions of the Anglican Communion as happening within this larger family, and to look to these 'parents' for ultimate authority in settling them. Laud's is a helpful enlargement of the perhaps rather twentieth century picture we find in the 1978 Lambeth Conference's description of a family likeness between the member Churches of the Anglican Communion (a likeness 'which is other than uniformity, but is nonetheless strong enough to hold them together in the midst of strain and tension'),[7] with its echoes of the stresses of the modern Western small family unit.

The changes in Anglican life and practice have accelerated in the last two centuries and especially as a direct result of the expansion beyond the provinces of Canterbury, York, Armagh and Dublin brought about by missionary endeavour.[8] 'At the date of the first Lambeth Conference, 1867,' said the Conference of 1920, 'this Communion had taken the form of a federation of self-governing Churches, held together for the most part without legal sanctions by a common reverence for the same traditions and a common use of a Prayer Book ... the Anglican Communion of today is a federation of Churches, some national, some regional, but no longer predominantly Anglo-Saxon in race, nor can it be expected that it will attach special value to Anglo-Saxon traditions'.[9] This poses the question whether we should now attach importance to our common past, or seek to find in it a continuing bond. Perhaps the answer is that we should be finding that as our consciousness of the universality of the Church in our own day grows through ecumenical contacts and conversations, so must the awareness of the unity we share not only with earlier Anglicans but with all Christians in every age. And that cannot be realised without a self-knowledge and self-

[6] Laud, *Works* 2.346, Conference with Fisher.
[7] Lambeth, 1978, pp. 98-9.
[8] Lambeth, 1908, pp. 415-6, gives a list of new provinces at that date.
[9] Lambeth, 1920, p. 122, cf. Lambeth, 1948, p. 82.

awareness in which the consciousness of the consensus of history must play a substantial part.

When Anglicans have asked themselves since the sixteenth century who they are, they have answered consistently that they are catholic as well as reformed Christians. William Beveridge (1637-1708) says that 'the doctrine of our Church was so reformed that it agrees exactly with God's holy Word, as understood and interpreted by his whole Catholic Church'.[10] At the Lambeth Conference of 1930 a committee reports, 'Our ideal is nothing less than the Catholic Church in its entirety'.[11]

Nevertheless, since the sixteenth century Anglicans have formed a distinct ecclesial community which has not been in communion with various other ecclesial communities. This was seen in the sixteenth and seventeenth centuries to be not paradoxical at all, because it was regarded as a result of a deliberate breaking away by others: first by the Roman Catholic Church and later by dissenters among English protestants. 'We have not at all separated ourselves from the communion of the Catholic Church', argues John Bramhall (1594-1663).[12] Richard Baxter (1615-91) pleaded in treatise after treatise for peace and reunion between Anglicans and nonconformists. We are beginning in our own time to get beyond the habit of looking for blame and calling one another schismatics. With the benefit of hindsight, the Lambeth Conference of 1930 was already able to see the developments which created the Anglican Communion as a 'situation caused by the divisions of Christendom' and Anglicanism itself as 'in some sense an incident in the history of the Church Universal'.[13]

This is an important shift of perspective. It has made it possible for each separated Church no longer to see itself as the sole true and catholic Church, to which others must return, but as part of the universal Church, sharing catholicity even in broken or impaired communion. Bramhall saw Anglican catholicity as participating in the continuity of the universal Church in exactly this way. The Ecclesia Anglicana, as *apostolica* and holding the *antiquissima fides*,[14] the most ancient faith, is, he says, 'before the Reformation' and after 'as much the same Church, as a garden, before it is weeded and after it is weeded, is the same garden'.[15] He also thought it

---

10 William Beveridge, *Thesaurus Theologicus, Works* (Oxford, 1847), 10.604. On 'Catholic but reformed', see Lambeth, 1888, p. 171 and Lambeth, 1948, p. 83.

11 Lambeth, 1930, Committee Report on the Anglican Communion (2), p. 245.

12 Bramhall, *Vindication*, p. 96.

13 Lambeth, 1930, p. 245.

14 Lancelot Andrews (1555-1626), *Opuscula* (Oxford, 1852), p. 96, says that the *Ecclesia Anglicana* has the *antiquissima fides* and is *apostolica (Tortura Torti, Responsio* 45 and 69; *Ad Apologiam Card, Bellarmini,* 39).

15 Bramhall, *Vindication*, p. 113.

important that the Thirty-Nine Articles contain no anathemas. Anglicans have not put up walls and 'do not deny the being of any Church whatsoever, ... nor possibility of salvation in them'.[16]

This essential catholicity through time and across existing boundaries makes the Anglican Communion 'in its present character' provisional. The Lambeth bishops of 1930 'forecast the day when the racial and historical connections which at present characterize' the Anglican Communion 'will be merged in a larger fellowship in the Catholic Church'.[17] The Conference's Encyclical Letter says that 'it is our duty to envisage the one Church of Christ as it will be when reunited, and to shape the Churches of our own Communion so that they will, even now, conform as much as possible to that ideal, and be ready to take their place within it, when it is realised'.[18] The Encyclical Letter of 1958 sustains a vision of 'a united Church, Catholic and Evangelical, but no longer in the limiting sense of the word, Anglican'.[19] This picture of an 'until then' Anglicanism[20] should not now be frightening. It in no way implies that there is not an Anglican character worth preserving in a future united Church, or that Anglicanism is not ecclesially a valuable reality. The ecumenical endeavour is to enable each community to bring its own gifts and become more fully itself, as happens in good human relationships, and supremely in the reconciliation of the soul with God. It is in this confidence that there is nothing to be lost and everything to be gained that we go forward into this extended identity. That is to say, in the faith that what we are seeing in our own time is an awakening understanding of the catholicity of fellowship or *koinonia* to which Christians are called in a future united Church. That is the vision to which the last chapter of this study looks.

---

[16] *Ibid.*, p. 197.

[17] Lambeth, 1930, p. 246. When first mooted this was a motion regarded with some suspicion. William Goode berates those who 'already venture to boast of our Church being in a transition state, out of which she will emerge clothed in what they call the garb of Catholicism', *Some Difficulties in the Late Charge of the Lord Bishop of Oxford*, (London, 1842), p. 6.

[18] Lambeth, 1930, p. 155.

[19] Lambeth, 1958, I.27.

[20] Lambeth, 1958, I.27.

Chapter Two

The Authority of Scripture

Scripture and the Church

Faith in Christ is not only trust and commitment but also the holding of a truth, of which Christ himself is the guarantee. That truth is held fast not only in the mind and heart of the believer but also in the community of which he is made a member through faith and by baptism. The Church is in part constituted by this maintaining of the faith[1] and it has been of enormous ecclesiological significance in recent ecumenical conversations that Christians of different communions have been able increasingly to recognise that they share a common faith.[2]

The faith was first expressed in the young Church by Jesus' followers, as they proclaimed his message and recorded what eye-witnesses remembered of his life and teaching. It has been accepted by Christians in every century that it was under the guidance of the Holy Spirit that the record gradually came to be written down and - over several generations - accepted by the whole community as the canon of Scripture.[3] Yet the authority of Scripture has sometimes been defined since the sixteenth century in what might be called 'disjunctive' terms, that is, as standing apart from, or even in opposition to, authority in the Church. That was the picture which presented itself to Luther and other reformers who thought that the institutional Church of their own day had become so corrupt that it could no longer properly be called the Church at all, and claimed that 'Scripture alone' was the basis of their faith.

This is a view which has continued to be important in its influence on the thinking of many protestants. Where the polemic of the sixteenth century West has not been an influence, Christians through the centuries have for the most part wanted to say that the authority of Christ is expressed in the words and experience of the community of his people, first and supremely in Scripture, but also in the continuing life of the Church. The difficulty lies in arriving at a shared, received understanding of the relation between

---

1   'To be part of the Church of Christ, we must hold fast to the truth which was given at the beginning', *The Nature of Christian Belief*, p. 5.

2   For example, *Niagara*, 3.

3   *The Nature of Christian Belief*, pp. 5-6.

the first and second of these processes. For once the canon of Scripture was settled, Scripture's relationship to the Church was set on a new footing. The Church now had a task of stewardship of an existing 'Scripture'. Article 20 of the Thirty-Nine Articles describes the Church as 'witness and keeper' (*testis et conservatrix*). The single 'witness of the Church in the Scriptures' of the apostolic period became a joint witness of Church and Scripture in the continuing life of the Church and that is where from time to time problems have arisen about their relationship.

It can perhaps best be described as a relationship of mutual service. The Bible had and has 'a controlling authority', so that 'we need to place ourselves continually under the Scriptures if we are to draw on the grace of the truth of God which brings salvation, and to grow in Christlikeness'.[4] But the community has well-defined work to do in maintaining and holding fast to the truth once and for all delivered (Jude 3). It has to preserve the purity of the test of Scripture and transmit it uncorrupted to future generations. This 'keeping' of the text was a formidable responsibility in the circumstances of a persecuted early Church, and remained so throughout the centuries before the invention of printing. There is also a responsibility for translating the text into the languages spoken by the faithful once the original Greek and Hebrew were no longer enough. The late mediaeval Church in the West put its duty as 'keeper' before its duty as 'witness' here, and clung to the Latin translation which had been made by Jerome in the fourth century. Reformers from before the time of Wyclif[5] pressed the importance of enabling Scripture to speak to God's people for itself in the vernacular.

The 'witnessing' of the Church was talked of quite uncontroversially for many centuries in terms of making explicit what is implicit in what Scripture says, and discovering practical applications in the lives of individuals. This was the purpose of the 'allegorical' and 'anagogical' interpretations, which pointed to deeper, spiritual meanings; and of the 'tropological' or 'moral' interpretations which pointed out what the Christian ought to do to live as God intended him to. There was also a proper and continuing anxiety to correct interpretations which were at variance with orthodox faith.

These labours produced a vast body of exegetical literature by the end of the Middle Ages, much of it originating in the sermons of the Fathers. But the homiletic pattern of the Church's 'witnessing' underwent a major change during the last mediaeval centuries. A type of academic Latin sermon came into being in the early thirteenth century which imposed a highly formalised

---

4   *Ibid.*, p. 6.
5   Anne Hudson, *The Premature Reformation* (Oxford University Press, 1988).

pattern of division and subdivision of a theme. Although there was close
analysis of Scriptural texts within this framework, the old style of
systematic commentary on the text itself had been lost to the university
lecture-room, where it was now primarily an academic exercise. Sermons
in the vernacular became divorced from the context of the liturgy and were
heavily influenced by the formal Latin 'art of preaching', with two
differences. Preachers liked to use illustrative stories, often drawn from the
classics or other secular sources. And there was a tendency (especially
among the preaching friars) towards what in the eighteenth century would
have been called 'hell-fire' sermons. At this date, they were designed to
make the faithful aware of their obligation to confess their sins to priests
and do penance to escape the pains of punishment after death.

What the reformers missed in all this was solid, Biblically-based teaching
in a ministry of the Word within the regular worship of the community. It
was argued by Luther that the Church was abusing its authority and
imposing its own innovations on the faithful in the guise of preaching, and
that it was urgently necessary to return to a clear Biblical basis. The
relationship of mutual service in which Scripture and the Church ought to
stand appeared to have broken down in this key area.[6]

These 'impositions' were seen in some cases as additions to Scripture's
teaching, and in others as contradicting it. But in both instances they were
attacked for being of human devising and without divine warrant. They
were also felt to take away the right of the individual Christian to make his
or her personal response to the Holy Spirit's moving, independent reading
of Scripture. There was, in other words, a complex sense of resentment
among the reformers about the abuse of authority by ecclesiastical power.

It is possible to begin to unravel it by looking at the late mediaeval and
sixteenth century understanding of the relationship of the 'once and for all'
and the 'continuing'; that is of the way a truth given once and for all in
Christ and recorded definitively in the text of Scripture can be compatible
with the picture of the Holy Spirit forever breaking through old habits of
thought with a fresh vision. 'Renewal' of this sort was less important in
earlier thinking than that fixity of the truth of which Archbishop Whitgift
(c.1530-1604) said, 'there is but one truth and that is certain'.[7] The
majority of mediaeval scholars - including Wyclif - assume that one and the
same truth was taught by Christ and the apostles, by the Fathers and by the
General Councils, and that it was not only right (*recta*) but also the same for

6 J.J. Murphy, *Mediaeval Rhetoric: A Bibliography* (Toronto, 1971) gives a convenient
   conspectus of literature on mediaeval preaching.
7 Whitgift, Cartwright, p. 44.

every age (*eadem*).[8] There was little sense of historical change or cultural difference to give these thinkers a contextual perspective.[9] For Nowell, in his Catechism of 1570, 'it were a point of intolerable ungodliness and madness to think, either that God had left an imperfect doctrine, or that men were able to make that perfect which God left imperfect'.[10] Any statement of a truth given once and for all in a way appropriate to a new age seemed to him and others among the reformers to involve addition or change, and above all the implication that God had not given all that was needed for salvation in Scripture itself.

The Thirty-Nine Articles address this debate by describing Scripture as containing all that is 'necessary to salvation'.[11] That is to say, they make a distinction between essentials contained in Scripture, and other points of belief which are 'not to be required of any man' to be 'believed as an article of Faith' or 'thought requisite or necessary to salvation' (Article 6). On the other hand, they allow this 'containing' to include both what is 'read therein' and what 'may be proved thereby', that is, both what is explicitly stated in Scripture and what is in some degree implicit. Understood in this way, Scripture is said to be 'sufficient' for salvation.

The notion of Scripture as containing what is 'necessary to salvation' was nothing new. A debate on the subject was in full flow in Aquinas three hundred years earlier. But its particular thrust in the sixteenth century was different. It concerned the role the Church could play in the salvation of the individual. Luther's contention was that the Church played no part at all except as servant of the Word, in other words, through her ministry of the Word which alone brought the sinner to saving faith. He saw the ministry of the sacraments as standing under that ministry and as salvific only by the power of the Word. The Anglican article sidesteps certain questions (which are not resolved in the Lutheran debates either): whether it is the content of the faith taught in Scripture which is crucial here (the knowledge of the facts of faith (*notitia*) which is shared even by devils[12]); and whether what Scripture tells the Christian to 'do' is include in what is 'necessary for salvation'.

Anglican authors after the sixteenth century returned to the principle that Scripture contains all that is 'necessary to salvation'. John Ellis wrote in 1696 in support of the view that the Church is minister of the Word in a

---

8   Wyclif, *De Ecclesia*, ed. J. Loserth (London, 1886) p. 112.

9   Peter Abelard's *Sic et Non* of the mid-twelfth century is a notable exception (*Patrologia Latina* 178).

10   Nowell, *Catechism*, PS, p. 115.

11   The phrase is repeated in the Lambeth Quadrilateral of 1888.

12   This was the subject of a series of debates at Wittenberg from the 1530s; see Luther, Weimar Ausgabe 39$^{i\text{-}ii}$.

way which makes it dependent for its authority on what Scripture allows.
'The Church does not have supreme and principal authority in settling
controversies of faith', he said, 'but a ministerial and limited authority'
(*ministerialis et limitata*).[13] Daniel Waterland (d.1740) suggested that
within the 'essentials of the Christian fabric or system' there is room to
allow for individual capacities and limitations in defining what is 'ordinarily
necessary to salvation'. Veneer (1730) suggested that to say that Scripture
contains all that is necessary to salvation is tantamount to saying that 'we
have such general Rules in Scripture, as may be applied to all cases that may
happen'.[14]

There appears to have been no consistent understanding that Article 6
implied the exclusion of a ministerial office for the Church in interpreting
and applying what Scripture says in her capacity as 'witness'. Herbert
Thorndike (d.1672) saw that 'to be necessary to salvation is to be true and
something more'.[15] It is thus to 'contribute' to the believer's salvation. So
it has been argued generation by generation by Anglican writers that the
salvific role of the Church is inseparable from a ministry of the Word
which is part of that 'something more'. In the later nineteenth century Ball
puts this apostolic task in this way. He says that the office of the Holy Spirit
in the Church has been 'to enable the Apostles to understand truths already
revealed to them'. 'Consequently,' he goes on, the authority of the Church
in matters of faith is declarative and definitive, not strictly 'prescriptive' or
in any sense 'originative'.[16] Nothing is added. But something is unfolded.
It is a matter of 'showing forth', 'proclaiming', says the 1968 Lambeth
Conference.[17] There is 'not a continuous revelation, but a continuous
interpretation'.[18] The Church's pronouncements play a 'limited but creative
role' in this way, in 'defining what is that faith which is uniquely revealed in
the Scriptures'.[19]

It has become increasingly clear in modern times that this 'showing forth'
can never be finished in a world which changes, and where language and
attitudes continually evolve. The fears of the sixteenth century on both sides
encouraged a tendency to try in effect to set artificial limits to the direction

---

[13] John Ellis, *Articulorum XXXIX Ecclesiae Anglicanae Defensio* (Amsterdam, 1696), p.
75.

[14] Veneer, p. 164.

[15] Thorndike, p. 24.

[16] Ball, p. 121.

[17] Lambeth, 1968, pp. 82-3.

[18] H.R. McAdoo, 'The influence of the seventeenth century on contemporary Anglican
understanding of the purpose and functioning of authority in the Church', *Christian
Authority*, p. 253.

[19] *The Nature of Christian Belief*, p. 7, speaking of the Creeds.

and guidance of the Holy Spirit: the Roman Catholic Church by seeking to keep to the Vulgate; and the protestant reformers by seeking to isolate the study of Scripture from the collective witness of the community and place it primarily in the hands of individuals. In the confidence that there is no need to fear that there will be any 'adding' or 'contradicting' in the long term, the Lambeth Conference of 1968 spoke of 'a concept of authority which refuses to insulate itself against the testing of history and the free action of reason'.[20]

Nevertheless, suspicion of an authority of the Church as set over against an authority of Scripture has continued to be a serious concern in those protestant Churches which identified themselves in the sixteenth century as standing on 'Scripture alone'.[21] Paradoxically such Communions may now find themselves defending their own 'tradition', that is, the way in which they have 'developed their thinking, worship, common life and attitudes to the world' as an ecclesial body.[22] If a sense of 'identity' like this is felt to be at stake, that can present a serious barrier to ecumenical progress. The understanding of tradition which these debates in the Western Church have encouraged, needs to be set here in the wider context which Orthodox experience provides.

In an Anglican-Orthodox agreement of 1976 it was affirmed 'that Scripture is the main criterion whereby the Church tests traditions to determine whether they are truly part of Holy Tradition or not' and 'that Holy Tradition completes Holy Scripture in the sense that it safeguards the integrity of the Biblical message'. The Holy Tradition is defined here not as teaching and pronouncements alone, but as ' the entire life of the Church in the Holy Spirit'. 'This tradition expresses itself in dogmatic teaching, in liturgical worship, in canonical discipline, and in spiritual life. These elements together manifest the single and indivisible life of the Church'.[23] Seen in this way as the very common life of the community which is the

---

[20] Lambeth, 1968, p. 82. Sixteenth century Anglican authors were especially preoccupied with 'unwritten tradition' and the question whether it could have equal authority with the written Scriptures' and with the notion that any tradition of the Church's 'making' could be sustained as equal with Scripture. See, for example, Tyndale, 3.26 and 96-100, PS, and Rogers, p. 78, PS.

[21] A-L. Pullach 38, *Growth*, p. 18. There is not and has never been a distinctively Anglican position on this matter. The Anglican Communion and its theologians have spoken with the times, on what has always been an issue of universal importance in the Church.

[22] A-L. Pullach, 33-4.

[23] A-O, Moscow, 1976, 10, *Growth*, p. 42.

body of Christ, tradition cannot be thought to stand in opposition to Scripture which is the guide and rule of that life.[24]

Tradition, Reason and Experience

It is sometimes suggested that it is characteristically Anglican to arrive at an understanding on the basis of Scripture, tradition, reason and experience.[25] But when we look into this claim, we find Anglicans participating in a much larger and more complex and widespread exercise. The place of 'reason' in Christian decision-making was controversial from the beginning. It was axiomatic for those with a philosophical training in the Roman world that the distinguishing mark of a man is, as Aristotle says, his capacity for rational thought, and that it is as a reasoning being that man most closely resembles his Creator.[26] At the same time there was recurring anxiety about the dangers of letting the philosopher run free in his thinking, and about the related question of the place of a secular scientific learning in Christian tradition.[27] It seemed that a rational being ought to have been able to arrive at the truths of faith if he used his God-given faculties properly; but experience showed that he was liable to go wrong. That was because his thinking was clouded by sin, Augustine of Hippo (354 - 430) suggested.[28]

Anselm, Archbishop of Canterbury (1033 - 1109), thought it possible to trust the powers of human reason to come to sound conclusions. Anselm demonstrates again and again throughout his writings that as a reasoning being he has no difficulty with the primacy of Scripture. When he deploys an argument from reason he pauses before continuing, to show what he has said accords with Scripture. In the *De Concordia* (III.6) he explains that nothing which Scripture does not contain, implicitly or explicitly, is conducive to salvation. If reason sometimes leads us to make a statement which cannot be found in so many words in Scripture, he says that we must look to see if it can be proved by reference to Scripture. Even if that is not at first sight possible, we can still apply a Scriptural test. If it is clearly reasonable, and Scripture in no respect contradicts it, we may infer that it is

24 The first Anglican-Roman Catholic Commission saw the difference between a view of tradition as 'an unfolding of the riches of the original revelation' and a picture of it as 'the growth of the seed of God's Word from age to age', as one of different emphasis. 'Neither approach is immune from the possibility of error', it admits. See ARCIC A I, Elucidation 2, *Growth*, p. 101.

25 See for example, J.E. Booty, 'The judicious Mr. Hooker', Sykes, pp. 94 ff.

26 *The Cambridge History of Later Greek and Early Mediaeval Philosophy*, ed. A.H. Armstrong provides a reliable guide.

27 *Ibid.*

28 See G.R. Evans, *Augustine on Evil* (Cambridge, 1983).

supported by Scripture's authority, for Scripture leaves no room for error without indicating that it is error. If Scripture is found to oppose our reasoning, even if that reasoning seemed to us to be unassailable, we must let it go as false. So Scripture contains within it the authority for all truths which may be arrived at by reason.[29] Less optimistic authors than Anselm, some of them confronting Jewish or Moslem or dissident or 'dualist' controversialists, and thus endeavouring to make reason serve where the authority of the Old or New Testament, or indeed of the whole of Scripture, was not acceptable, struggled throughout the Middle Ages with the respective roles of reason and revelation in establishing theological truths.

In the late sixteenth century, Hooker suggested that although 'naturall light, teaching morall virtues, teacheth things necessarie to salvation', yet it cannot do so perfectly without the aid of revelation, 'that supernaturall knowledge' revealed in Scripture.[30] He places reason under Scripture in a graded list of proofs in order of 'firmness'. Scripture is most compelling because it comes directly from God. Beneath it Hooker places 'intuitive beholding', the intellectual instinct by which we recognise what is self-evidently true; then 'strong and invincible demonstration' to which 'the mind doth necessarily assent' because it rests upon self-evident truths.[31] Lowest comes 'probability'.[32] This grading of proofs by reasoning follows a standard mediaeval pattern. But Hooker draws into it a series of preoccupations of his own centuries: especially the notions of 'judgement' and 'knowledge' and 'discretion'. 'The first mean whereby nature teacheth men to judge good from evil, as well in laws as in other things', he says, 'is the force of their own discretion'.[33] Such discretion needs instruction. While it is true that the people should not obey their leaders blindly and without consulting their consciences, it is equally important for them not to assert 'rules' or 'truths' where they do not have the knowledge.[34] Only informed judgement can arm the faithful against 'inducements' used to make certain ideas 'saleable' to them.[35] Knowledge, got both from life and from study, must underpin judgement. Hooker says that everyone 'from the

---

[29] Anselm's works are edited by F.S. Schmitt (Rome-Edinburgh 1938-68), 6 vols. The point is made again in *De Processione Spiritus Sancti*, 14.

[30] Hooker, *A Christian Letter*, p. 11.

[31] These belong to the demonstrative method derived in part from Aristotle's *Posterior Analytics* and exemplified in Euclid's *Elements*. On the mediaeval tradition, see the article by E. Serene in *The Cambridge History of Later Mediaeval Philosophy*, ed. N. Kretzmann *et al.* (Cambridge, 1982), pp. 496 ff.

[32] Hooker, *Laws* III.vii.5.

[33] *Laws*, Preface III.1.

[34] *Ibid.*, III.4.

[35] *Ibid.*, III.5.

greatest to the least' must 'be able for every several article' of their belief
'to show some special reason as strong as their persuasion'.[36] In the
eighteenth century we find a series of treatises comparing proofs from
reason with proofs from revelation. It is with something of this background
in mind that we must read such statements as Thorndike's in 1845 that
reason is both illuminating, and a means of 'evidencing what God's
messengers have delivered to us', and that 'reason' can 'make clear' those
things 'necessary to salvation' which are not 'clear in the Scriptures of
themselves, but by consequence of reason';[37] and the volumes of the
nineteenth and twentieth centuries which discuss the place of 'scientific'
proving in establishing truths of faith.

This preoccupation with weighing one form of authority against another,
and the heritage which encourages us to speak of a 'witness', should not be
allowed to encourage a limited or forensic notion of 'proving'. There is no
trial with the accused in the dock. There is certainly a place, and an
important place, for 'proving' Christian truth, but 'proving' means 'testing
and experiencing' as well as 'demonstrating'. Scripture is in part an
exception to the rule that our sources of authority are secondary to the
divine Author whose gift they are, because although it comes to us through
human authors, Christians accept its divine authorship as the Word of God.
But its humanity is, as Augustine and Gregory the Great saw, an inseparable
element in it, and perhaps one of God's greatest gifts in Scripture.
Scripture's authority works in some measure through human experience in
the life of the community. 'Experience' was another commonplace of
discussion in and before Aquinas and by no means a peculiarly Anglican
'source;. It needs to be taken in conjunction with a full conspectus of other
tests, suggested Newland in 1829. He saw, as did Veneer in 1730, that
experience can otherwise be an unreliable guide.[38] Hooker warns against
putting too much reliance on that aspect of experience which has to do with
feelings. 'When men's affections do frame their opinions, they are in
defence of error more earnest ... than (for the most part) sound believers in
the maintenance of truth apprehended according to the nature of that
evidence which Scripture yieldeth'.[39] In our own period Bicknell stresses
that experience is a process of verification of truths which is 'not only

---

[36] *Ibid.*, III.10.
[37] Thorndike, pp. 18 and 24.
[38] Newland, p. 97; cf. Veneer, 1730, p. 135. Newland's comment is that 'experience
shows that tradition tends to the corruption of truth' unless it is taken in conjunction with
a full conspectus of sources and tests.
[39] *Laws*, Preface III.10.

intellectual but moral and spiritual', a matter of 'learning the reasons for beliefs'.[40]

It is important, then, not to over-simplify the picture of a distinctive Anglican reliance on Scripture, tradition, reason, experience, in decision-making. Anglican thinkers have been the children of their times in their comments on these means of establishing authoritativeness. Something at once simpler and profoundly more difficult to fix, is in practice the test most usually applied: that is, consonance with Scripture. This is a 'consentient witness', as Tyrrell Green felicitously describes it in the nineteenth century.[41] It has to do with being 'in accordance with God's Word',[42] with being 'agreeable to the ... Scriptures'.[43] It involves a principle with a sound mediaeval pedigree[44] and also to be found in the sixteenth century Articles (Article 5 of 1552), in the reference to *ordo et decor*: that 'harmony' and 'fittingness' are a test of truth in matters of faith. That is not to make a cloud of witnesses Scripture's equals. But the primacy of Scripture is not threatened by acknowledging that no witness can support itself, in logic or in law. The task of maintaining Scripture's teaching and 'keeping' the text itself has always fallen to the Church, and to individuals within the Church, working in harness and in co-operation with Scripture. The test of consonance with Scripture allows Scripture to remain the unique and absolute standard, while giving a real working place to the intellectual and spiritual endeavour of the Christian community. Thus the Fathers, to whom as the sixteenth century wore on English reformers turned for authority,[45] and the sixteenth century Anglican formularies themselves, like 'official' and private documents of all sorts in every age, may be seen as authoritative, not in their own right, but insofar as they are recognisably consonant with Scripture.

Of course that begs many questions. It has not always been the case that one body of Christians could recognise that consonance, in a text which appeared to others to be wholly in agreement with Scripture. That was conspicuously so in the sixteenth century, when Lutherans pointed, for example, to the Augsburg Confession, and Roman Catholics perhaps to a papal decree. In what follows, I have tried to use the sources in a common-sense manner, not forcing them, but letting them speak for themselves as far

---

[40] Bicknell, p. 250.

[41] Tyrrell Green, p. 140.

[42] Goode, p. 12.

[43] Canon A 5.

[44] The theme of 'fittingness' is of central importance in the thought of Anselm of Canterbury in particular.

[45] See S.L. Greenslade, 'The English Reformers and the Councils of the Church', *Oecumenica*, 1967.

as possible; and above all, seeking to place them in the context of the full living witness of the life of the Church throughout the ages. Many problems of methodology in the use of sources are glossed over in such an approach. But it is doubtful whether they can be resolved satisfactorily as yet in any systematic way. Anglicans and the protestant Churches in general cannot point to a corpus of texts authorised by a unified ecclesial structure from the beginning. In a future united church it may be possible for all Christians to enter more fully into that heritage. But as a working method for present ecumenical purposes it may be that we cannot do better than appeal to consensus about Scripture; we could certainly do no worse than seek in this way to hold what is in harmony with the apostolic faith.

Chapter Three

The Church's Order and Structures

It is one thing to seek to describe the structures of authority which have emerged in the history of the Church, and another to try to make an authoritative statement about the working of Christian authority. Before that can be attempted, it is necessary to seek to answer questions of another order, about the authority on which authoritativeness is to be judged. There is some unavoidable moving from level to level in what follows because it must be asked of every system not only 'does it meet the needs of Christians here and now?' (is it practically right?), but also 'is it in harmony with what we understand to be Christian authority?' (is it theologically right?) It is particularly important to be aware of this difficulty in writing about authority in a single Communion because of the danger of blurring distinctions between theological questions - which are not peculiar to Anglicans - and matters of especially Anglican concern in the running of the Churches of the Anglican Communion.

The assumptions of our own or any other time unavoidably give a subtle shading to any attempt to characterise Christian authority. All Christians can agree that the source of Christian authority is divine; that the Father sent the Son into the world with authority as Lord. We can see that Christ's authority is never cut off from its source, but flows into the world perpetually in the continuing life of the people of God, making all Christians its channels in different ways. But if we go on to say that the Bible reveals God as at once all-powerful and yet giving his children freedom to challenge him,[1] we are speaking a language which we should have to translate for Christians of an earlier age if they were to recognise it in their own faith. That does not mean that we are not getting it right, but it ought to alert us to the need to be conscious of the assumptions we are making, and of our adoption of present-day habits of thought. We have, in other words, a responsibility to think universally in terms of time as well as place; and in terms of past cultural differences as well as present-day ones.

With that caveat, we must try now to set out the basics of the notion of Christian authority with which this study works. God's absolute power and goodness stand behind. God is never coercive. He encourages mankind to

---

[1] This is a theme of the work of Stephen Sykes. See, too, Resp. 216.

express pain and puzzlement as Job did. He prompts the movement of the
Church out into the world in imitation of his own loving response to human
need. There the Church has freedom to discover what works best in a given
situation, to be open to change, within the framework of God's purpose.
What God desires for his Church is that it may find itself in free conformity
with his will, which is the ground of its being. The characteristics of
Christ's own exercise of authority are the model for the exercise of
authority in the Church.[2] He who is Lord of all came as the servant of
people's needs. He made no compromise with wrong but he showed infinite
compassion for the sinner. He compelled no-one to come to him, but he
attracted multitudes. On the Cross he exerted no coercive power, but his
authority there reached its highest expression.[3] The power which is lodged
in the Church must, then, be the paradoxical 'power of the crucified',[4] and
that makes it at once fully human and fully divine in its strength in weakness
(Ephesians 4), reflecting both the lordship and the service of Christ
(Ephesians 4; Philippians 2.11). It is worth labouring this point at the
outset, because most of the problems which have arisen about the exercise of
authority in the Church through the ages have been provoked by the
suspicion that the lordship was outweighing the service.

Among the sixteenth century Homilies of the Church of England is a
sermon 'Concerning good order'. It links the 'most excellent and perfect
order' of 'all things in heaven' and of the created natural world with order
in human society; and it goes on to draw a disturbing picture of the
consequences of a breakdown in that order.[5] Its immediate purpose is to
encourage good citizenship and submission to the civil authorities (cf.
Article 37). But it draws on an older understanding of the governing
system of the universe than its concern with sixteenth century questions of
princely government and proper jurisdiction suggest. It had been self-
evident to generations of Christian thinkers since the ancient world that
eternal harmony is built into the created structures of the world and into
our humanity, as natural law. Earthly law, or order, is an appropriation of
that order by human beings as intelligent creatures responding to the
contingencies of life, and, in the case of Christian order, this 'appropriation'
is understood to be guided by the Holy Spirit. Such ideas were explored as
fully by Aquinas in the thirteenth century as by Hooker.

As God intends it, eternal order is a harmony in which all things are held
in balance and proportion without chafing or tugging. Where all do the best
for all in love, authority need never constrain. Yet order in the Church in

2   Resp. 217.
3   Cf. Emmaeus, p. 65.
4   Resp. 216.
5   The Anglican Homilies, p. 72.

this world has work to do because of human frailty. We need 'ordered
structures' which are designed to protect and safeguard because we are
imperfect in love.[6] If the authority of heaven may be seen as an electrical
potential, authority on earth will sometimes need to run as a current,
potestas to issue in *actus*, in ways which are in accordance with God's
purpose for his created order. As well as being active, such this-worldly
ordering will necessarily be provisional, in three senses: it will have
reference to needs which will not be the same in the life to come (sacrament
or rule will be fulfilled and transformed); it will be in part mutable
(although divine and natural law endure, human law can change, and so at
the practical level no arrangement in Church government can be regarded
as permanent); it will be imperfect.

All this makes structures a necessity, as instruments of authorising. As
T.I. Ball put it a century ago, 'A society of men cannot exercise any
authority that belongs to it *in confuso;* it must exercise it through the proper
officers of the society'.[7] Three areas of great controversy have arisen in
this connection. The first concerns the style of such 'exercising' of
authority, whether it is to compel obedience or constitute any kind of
dominion; whether it should resemble contemporary political government in
its shape and methods of administration. The second has to do with the
particular types of 'officer' the 'society' of the Church should have. The
third involves the relationship between the ministry of the whole people of
God and the ministry of these 'officers'.

The particular reservation we are likely to bring to the question of order
in the Church in an anti-authoritarian age is a resistance to any suggestion of
dominion or coercion, the sort of language used at the end of the
seventeenth century by George Hickes (1642-1715), in the heat of a
contemporary controversy, when he asserted that bishops had power in New
Testament times 'to coerce or compel their subjects ... to obey them', that
they were 'spiritual princes' and 'their dioceses principalities'.[8] The
difficulty is not to conceive of, but to keep in balance in practice, a pattern
of exercise of authority in the Church in which obedience and co-operation
are not in opposition but in harness, and obedience is thus free of
associations of tyranny. Yet that is the model which emerges from the New
Testament.[9]

In the sixteenth century the concern was not primarily with the objections
which might be made to rule or coercion as such in the Church, but to what

---

6   Resp. 217.
7   Ball, p. 123. Cf. Gundrum, pp. 2, 29.
8   Hickes, p. 301. He also saw episcopacy as 'tyrannical in its frame and constitution', pp.
    268-9.
9   M. MacDonald, *The Pauline Churches* (Cambridge University Press, 1988).

was seen as a 'clerical tyranny'. Thomas Erastus (1524-83) lent his name to
an 'Erastianism' which reversed the tendency since the eleventh century to
insist that spiritual authority is supreme over temporal power. In
accordance with a policy of *cuius regio, eius religio*, we see German princes
at work, convening meetings, receiving books dedicated to them by
theologians, even lending their authority to theological statements. Papal
and episcopal and 'priestly' authority was challenged by reformers, but only
the Anabaptists and a few other extremist groups wanted to deny civil
authority. Zwingli spoke for the main body of the reforming movement
when he said that 'temporal' authority 'derives strength and affirmation
from the teaching and work of Christ', and that consequently all Christians
owe it obedience.[10]

In the circumstances in which the Church of England became divided
from Rome, a solid regard for the importance of secure and princely
government was inevitably much in the minds of Church leaders, and it
pervades the sixteenth century Anglican formularies. Whitgift (cf. 1530-
1604) stresses the primacy of 'the right government of the Church' in co-
operation with the government of the state. Only in this way, he argues, can
'confusion' and 'disorder' be avoided and, with it, the threat to 'princes,
magistrates and commonwealths'.[11] William Laud (1573-1646) declares that
the Church of England 'believes ... that our Saviour Christ hath left in his
Church, beside His law-book the Scripture, visible magistrates and judges -
that is, archbishops and bishops, under a gracious king, to govern both for
truth and peace according to the Scripture'.[12]

This contemporary view of the right and necessary association of Christ
and Caesar in the government of the Church carried with it at that time a
view of 'order' which was inseparable from a rather narrow conception of
hierarchy and degree as involving dominion and subjection. Whitgift's
opponent, the puritan Thomas Cartwright, speaks of 'degree and order one
under another', as though human hierarchy were as uncontroversial as
hierarchy in the created order; and indeed he saw it as simply a part of it.[13]
Political discussions carried over into discussions of the structures of order
in the Church even where the relations of Church and state were not at
issue.[14]

---

10 Zwingli, *Defence*, Articles 34, 35, 37.
11 Whitgift, Cartwright, p. 17 ff.
12 Laud, *Fisher*, p. 234.
13 Whitgift, Cartwright, p. 18. Cf. Cranmer, *Remains*, Appendix, p. 486, on episcopal
    potestas super alios.
14 Political and constitutional patterns have left their mark on Christian Church structures in
    a variety of ways, from those of Rome and the Byzantine world of the late classical and
    early mediaeval periods to the British Commonwealth of Nations and African tribal
    models in more recent Anglican experience. The Church of England presents a special

Here, as elsewhere, it is easy to see at a distance of time the way in which the preoccupations of the day marked the discussion, and contemporary vocabulary coloured it. In the discussions of the nineteenth century Lambeth Conferences the leading word would, for example, be 'duty', where today's talk would be of 'responsibility' and 'service'. Every age has its models. Today's danger is of seeking to replace a paternalistic or 'imperial' model with a crudely democratic one in which one imbalance supplants another; for democracy is not necessarily identical with 'fellowship', or the majority vote an expression of that consensus which must be unanimity. We shall come to some of the implications of this sort of exchange of assumptions as we go on. But we need to recognise them at the outset as variants of the fear of 'tyranny' which has always tended to bedevil discussions of the right place for governance within the Church, its style and mode of operation.

The puritan divine John Owen (1616-83) took a clear if schematic view of the alternatives. He contrasts what he calls the 'descending' and 'ascending' theories descending and ascending theoriesof the means by which a Church is constituted. 'To constitute a ... Church by descent, it must be supposed that all Church power is vested in ... officers, namely, archbishops, and from them derived ... by a distribution of power'. By the 'ascending' theory, we constitute a Church by becoming 'members by our own voluntary consent', in voluntary consentother words, by an ecclesiastical 'social contract'. social contract Owen's complaint was that the 'unity' of the Church of England as then constituted 'consists in the subjection of one sort of officers unto another'.[15] The emphasis of many centuries in the Church had been upon such 'descending' theories. The challenge of Waldensians in the twelfth century, and Lollards in the

case because its inception as a spearate ecclesial body involved the acceptance of the English monarchs as its Head (Henry VIII) or Governor (Elizabeth I). There was a strong sixteenth century concern to establish parallels between the structure of Parliament and the structure of the Convocation as a legislative body. For example, the Lower House of Convocation petitioned in 1547 that either they might be 'adjoined and associated with the Lower House of Parliament', as the Bishops were with the Lords, or else that 'all such statutes and ordinances, as shall be made concerning all matters of religion and causes ecclesiastical, may not pass without the sight and assent of the said clergy' (Cardwell, *Synodalia*, II.4221). The variability of such parallel structuring and its provisional character is clear enough from a comparison with the United States, where the model was the House of Deputies, in which clergy and laity were joined, and where it was intended that the episcopate should be wholly separate fromt he state, with no echo of the mediaeval 'prince-bishop' who survives int he modern British House of Lords (Gundrum, p. 2).

For material relating to other provinces, see the *Handbook of Anglican Sources*, ed. G.R. Evans and J. Robert Wright (SPCK, forthcoming).

[15] Owen, *Of Schism*, pp. 188, 197.

fifteenth, and of other groups of mediaeval dissidents, had consequently been to propose some form of voluntary association, with democratic government, as an alternative to it, rather than seeing that as a corrective to balance it. The call for 'Gospel freedom' in the sixteenth century was not for a truth unhampered by corrupt authority alone (or freedom from servitude to sin, which is perhaps its real meaning); it was also for a personal freedom in matters of faith which, it was felt, was being denied by existing Church government. The concern of the Anglicans who established the system of government for the Church in England under the Tudor monarchs was rather different. They sought to eliminate abuses from what they still found in principle to be an acceptable conception of Church government as properly 'descending' in its authority, and they did little to establish machinery by which a complementary 'ascending' authorising might act together with it.

Chapter Four

Authority in the Local Community

At baptism every Christian receives a commission for ministry,[1] which may
be fulfilled in a multitude of ways, according to gifts and circumstances.
All these ministries, taken collectively, make up the 'priesthood of all
believers', and all Christians share equally in this common priesthood
because it is a participating together in the unique priesthood of Christ.
This collective character of the priesthood of all believers was stressed by
some but not all of the sixteenth century reformers; many were spurred by
hatred of what they saw to be the arrogance of a clerical class to assert that
all Christians individually are priests as much as anyone who has been
ordained. Their main concern was to deny that ordination conferred any
special 'power'. In this they were heirs of Lollard and other mediaeval
dissidents who had consciously seen themselves as engaged in a power-
struggle here. Anticlericalism of this sort[2] presupposes an understanding of
ordination as conferring a personal power which the ordained ministry
subsequently exercises for life in its own right. That is a false picture. The
ordained minister is placed by ordination in a special relationship to the
common priesthood, on behalf of the community of which he has pastoral
charge. This is not a handing over of authority to be exercised as a personal
right, but an entrusting of responsibility answerable to Christ and to the
community. What is involved is a service to the community, and it is
always exercised from within the community and on its behalf, and thus it
can have no independent authority. Such an office is not an open-ended gift
of power, but an entrusting of authority for a limited purpose within the
koinonia, or fellowship.

All authority in the Church is both personal and corporate. The personal
presence of Christ is the means by which divine authorising acts in the
Church, and that personal presence within the whole body has from the
beginning been represented and focused within each community by the

---

1 Vatican II, II.iii.ii.47, 48; cf. Cardinal Suenens, *Coresponsibility in the Church*, English
   ed. (London, 1968); cf. Niagara, 17.
2 *Proceedings* of the General Synod of the Church of England, November, 1986, debate
   on *The Priesthood of the Ordained Ministry*, Board of Mission and Unity, 1986, brought
   out similar anxieties today.

leadership of the ordained ministry, in such a way that it is also corporate. On this understanding the arguments against the need for ordained ministry, on the grounds that it usurps a God-given right of all believers in favour of a few privileged individuals, look very different.

A second plea against the need for an ordained ministry within the Church has also recurred century by century. Here the problem is not that the liberty of the faithful is thought to be threatened, but that the freedom of divine grace seems to be compromised by institutionalisation which seeks to clip the wings of its power. The notion that bishops in particular might have been an extraordinary and temporary provision, needed only in the apostolic and sub-apostolic age, but having no place in the modern Church, was canvassed from the late Middle Ages. It led some reforming communities to do away with 'bishops' or 'ordination' altogether, at least for a time. Whitgift reflects on the argument that the apostles were in a unique position to witness to the words and deeds of Jesus and to his resurrection. No later successor could bear their eye-witness. 'I think,' he says, 'the apostolic function was extraordinary, in respect that it had for the time certain especial properties, as to bear witness of the resurrection of Christ, and of his ascension, which they did see with their eyes; also to plant and to found churches, likewise to go throughout the whole world. These, I say, were temporal and extraordinary; and so was the apostleship in this respect, but yet ordinary in respect of their chief function, which was to preach the gospel and govern the churches which they had planted'.[3] 'Whatsoever was extra-ordinary, as immediate mission, unlimited jurisdiction, and miraculous operations, that was not necessary to the perpetual regiment of the Church', argues Jeremy Taylor (1613-67), for if it had been, the Church could not have continued without them. Christ 'promised his perpetual assistance' not in these 'extraordinary powers and privileges', but in the 'ordinary office' of 'preaching, baptising, consecration, ordaining and governing. For these were necessary for the perpetuation of a Church'.[4] A little later, opposing the views of the Latitudinarian bishop Benjamin Hoadly, Wright preached an ordination sermon on 'The Rights of Christian Priesthood' in which he says, 'It will be granted that the Persons ... immediately commissioned by our Saviour to preach the Gospel, and exercise the other parts of the Apostolical Office, acted by Divine Authority; it must be said therefore that either they had Authority from Christ to commission others successively to ordain to the same offices, or else that the Power of exercising that Authority 'dy'd with

---

3   Whitgift, *Works*, PS I.471.
4   Taylor, *Episcopacy Asserted*, pp. 19-20.

them'.[5] Thus the dispute had the positive effect of helping to clarify what are the tasks of a continuing 'ordinary' apostolic office, that is, one which is an integral part of the Church's order.

The New Testament texts reveal that there was both a direct Spirit-inspired ministry, and a pattern of 'offices' within the community, though not yet one with a fully developed constitutional structure. Paul sends greeting to the 'bishops and deacons' at Philippi (Philippians 1.1). This is the only Pauline allusion, except in the later pastoral epistles to Timothy and Titus, to ministerial offices of a permanent sort in a local Church. Paul's main emphasis is upon the creative power of the Holy Spirit to infuse the life of the Church with both vitality and order. (I Corinthians 12-14 suggests that the vitality was sometimes more forceful than the order.) The point of importance here is that the Pauline texts nowhere suggest that there was any opposition between 'order' and 'charism', but rather that they were both necessary and both had a place in each community.[6]

The ministerial focus of the lives of these communities was Paul himself, as their apostle. The gentile Churches are living proof of his call to preach to the gentiles; their membership in the one universal Church which had its focus and the touchstone of its communion in the mother Church at Jerusalem, depends upon the authenticity of his apostolate (Galatians 2.1-10 and I Corinthians 9.1-2).[7] The personal character of an apostolic leadership was thus of the first importance from the beginning; although it seems that local churches often tended to respect itinerant teachers and prophets more than their familiar resident bishops and deacons. Perhaps that was natural enough.[8]

Although the continuance of a personal episcopal missionary and itinerant ministry is to be seen from time to time in the later history of the Church (the early Irish *episcopi vagantes*, for example, or Willibrord and Boniface in their seventh and eighth century missions from England to the Continent; or the nineteenth century European missionaries to Africa), after the apostolic period this became comparatively unusual except in parts of the world where Christianity had not yet reached. There the missionary behaved as a *pontifex* in the sense of 'bridge-maker' to those who had not yet been touched by the Gospel. But the role of the special ministry settled for the most part into an increasingly institutional pattern.

---

5   Wright, *The Rights of Christian Priesthood* (London, 1717), p. 4.
6   Paul did not see Christian authority in office as limiting freedom; rather the opposite (II Corinthians 1.24; 10.8).
7   See the essay by Henry Chadwick in *Preparatory Essays* for the 1978 Lambeth Conference.
8   Cf. *Didache*, 15.

Bishop, priest and deacon

The Church of England made no changes in its pattern of three-fold ministry of bishops, priests and deacons under the Tudor monarchs. World-wide Anglican tradition has retained this ministerial structure. The office of bishop has proved crucial here. It was recognised to be so in the Chicago-Lambeth Quadrilateral of 1888, which placed 'the historic episcopate' alongside Scripture, the Creeds and the Sacraments as the foursquare basis on which the Church rests. Much turns now, both ecumenically and within the Anglican Communion, upon the understanding of this ministry; it is also the case that the orders of priest and deacon are best understood in relation to it. So it has a pivotal place in the discussion of 'order' in what follows.

The title 'pastor' has been acceptable to almost all protestant Churches, used to describe a minister with special responsibilities, and not applicable to every member of the community because it is clear that not everyone can be the shepherd; there must also be a flock. The theme of 'shepherding' is strong in the New Testament. In the first Epistle of Peter to the gentile Churches of Asia Minor the 'presbyters' are instructed to model themselves on Christ, who is the Chief Shepherd (I Peter 5.2-4).[9] It seemed to Aquinas in the thirteenth century, at a high point for claims of episcopal dominion, that this call to be shepherd is the supreme vocation of a bishop, and the only one to which the Christian ought to aspire.[10]

This is a shepherding which, from the earliest days, has made the bishop the person in whom the three planes of the Church's life intersect: that which unites pastor and people in the local eucharistic community; the 'local and universal' plane which relates communities to one another in the wider Church; and that of continuity through time.

Yet the person who holds the pastoral office is himself a sheep of Christ's flock, who needs as much as any the benefit of pastoral care.[11] Although at his consecration as bishop he is asked 'Will you strive to fashion your own life and that of your household according to the way of Christ?'[12] and must strive to set an example of holiness, he does so as one who is himself a sinner, and who enters into the sufferings of others with them. At the same time, he is Christ's representative. Thus he is both a reconciled and reconciling person. Like Jeremiah, he is given an authority to speak and act (Jeremiah 1.9-10) as one who shares his people's pain, and endures their troubles with them, in 'close and sympathetic relations with both clergy and

---

9   Cf. John 21.15-17 and 1922 Doctrine Commission, p. 120.
10 Aquinas, ST II^{ii} q.185 a.1.
11 Cf. 1922 Doctrine Commission, p. 123.
12 Alternative Service Book of the Church of England.

laity'.[13] This is an incarnational ministry, and a ministry of the Cross, which always stands under Christ's unique High Priesthood of sinless self-giving.

The highest qualities are required of a bishop, and these are not only spiritual or supernatural, but include natural qualities of leadership and common sense (cf. I Timothy 3.3-7; Titus 1.6-9). The charism of the Spirit is able in this way to work through the orderly structures which secure the Church in the world by resident and reliable ministry in the local community. Such ideas were already well-developed in the highly influential *Regula Pastoralis* of the sixth century Pope Gregory the Great, which the English King Alfred the Great translated into English. Gregory places an emphasis on the importance of a bishop's leading a life of prayer and holiness, not seeking worldly glory in his office, but having a strong sense of the weight of responsibility which rests on him.[14] He underlines again and again the need for a two-fold balance: of the inward and spiritual and the outward and active, in the bishop's own life; and of justice with firmness, and mercy shown with humility, in his leadership. Thomas Becon (c.1513-67) explores the notion that the bishop is 'minister of Christ' because he is Christ's ambassador', 'dispensator of the mysteries of God, because he is God's steward, that is to say, 'communicator of the heavenly riches and most blessed treasures of God ... to such as the Lord hath committed to his spiritual charge'. This pastoral service which puts the bishop at the disposal of the community is, paradoxically, the essence of his role as 'overseer or superintendent' and it is thus that he wields the 'sword' which God has committed to him.[15]

Ignatius (c.35-c.107) describes the bonds of love which make the eucharistic community led by its bishop a local microcosm of the universal Church. He stresses the importance of the community's thinking and acting as one with their bishop. This is a free co-operation of those who are of 'one mind' and share 'one hope'.[16] Augustine saw himself as standing 'with' and 'among' his people as a bishop.[17] This is the ancient understanding of the means by which the bishop may be 'the servant, not the lord of souls' and 'conformable to the example of Christ, by humility, charity and care of his flock', as the Anglican Thomas Wilson (1663-1755) puts it.[18] The idea is underlined in the service of ordination of a bishop in the Church of

---

[13] Cf. 1922 Doctrine Commission, p. 123.

[14] Gregory the Great, *Regula Pastoralis*, I.i-iii.

[15] Becon, *Catechism*, PS, pp. 317-19. Becon refers to the 'spiritual sword' of the mediaeval controversy about the 'two swords' of Luke 22.49-51

[16] Ignatius, *To the Magnesians*, 7.

[17] *Enarrationes in Ps. 126, 3*, CCSL, 40.1858-9.

[18] Thomas Wilson, *Sacra Privata Works* (Oxford, 1870), V. pp. 64-5.

England's Alternative Service Book, where the bishop is called 'to work with' his people 'in the oversight of the Church'. This model of conjoined endeavour contains within it the sanction implicit in the idea of the shepherd as guide and protector. The bishop has no powers apart from the community within which he serves, and every member participates in his authoritative actions. When discipline is necessary, as it must be in a fallen community, the bishop exercises it in the interests of the preservation of the common bond of love and unity.

Archbishop Laud, writing in the seventeenth century, saw this authority as 'a thing of known use and benefit for the preservation of unity and peace in the Church' and 'settled in the minds of men from the very infancy of the Christian Church'; he notes that this was Jerome's opinion, although he 'was no great friend to bishops'.[19] This is a personal authority in the sense that it is exercised by an individual to whom it is entrusted within the framework of the law. But it is also corporate and communal, for there can be no legitimate action of the Church which is not corporate and communal, and the bishop derives his authority in discipline from the acceptance of his people as well as from Christ their Head. Obedience to one entrusted with the responsibility of oversight is thus an expression of loyalty to the fellowship. The bishop acts not in dominion but in the interests of an order which may be seen as 'love in regulative operation'.[20]

This is all part of the Church's life as a community which seeks to submit to Christ, and whose members ought to live with respect for one another's needs. The bishop's power to require compliance acts for the sake of peace and mutual love and the maintenance of the truth. The Lambeth Conference of 1978 described this double structure of personal, and corporate or communal authorising thus: God's authority to the Church involves all the people of God in responsibility and obedience. The bishop derives his authority from the Church, that is, from both Christ its Head and the members, who are the faithful. The bishop's authority is not to be exercised apart from the Church.[21]

During the first century there seems to have been some diversity in structure between different regions and local churches. In some - as at Ephesus (Acts 20.17) - spiritual leadership was in the hands of a group of elders or 'presbyters', under the overall authority of the apostle. On the other hand, the mother Church at Jerusalem had a single head, in the person of James, the Lord's brother. This 'monarchical' and apparently earliest form of pastorate could easily be fused with a presbyteral council, in which

---

19 *Conference with Fisher* VIII.xii.25, p. 194.
20 A-R, 82.
21 Lambeth, 1978, p. 76.

it would be natural enough for one man to be regarded as first among equals because of his seniority in age or wisdom, or because of his charismatic powers, or because, like Stephanas at Corinth (I Corinthians 16.15-16), he was the first convert who formed a community about him. In the Pastoral Epistles to Timothy and Titus, presbyters are usually plural, with a single bishop; we may be seeing here an indication that in colleges of presbyters exercising pastoral oversight or *episcope* one is the commonly accepted president. Elsewhere things may have moved the other way, with a single pastor being joined, as the community grew, by a council of presbyter-helpers. But in either development there was no question of a loss of any sense of the person who exercised oversight fully sharing a common pastorate and liturgical functions with presbyteral colleagues. The twenty-four elders of Revelation 4.4 are sitting in a common council. If the basic pattern was one of primacy among equals, it is probable that in some places the equality was more in evidence than the primacy; in other places it might be the other way round. The bishop is certainly nowhere *less* than a presbyter. All this suggests that the early Church learnt by experience that the congregation and the group of congregations which form a diocese needs one man rather than a committee to act as its focus of unity.[22] The *Didache* or church order, probably of the first century mentions bishops (15); so does the epistle written from Rome by its bishop Clement of Rome about the end of the first century.[23] Ignatius of Antioch speaks strongly of what has come to be known as the 'monarchical' episcopate. What he says may be taken to underline not a juridical or dogmatic principle, but a practical need for the expression of unity. The Church certainly does not depend for its *being* upon having a personal episcopate; but in the greater part of the Christian world for most of its history it has found that it works.

All this is helpful in clarifying the basis of the traditional three-fold ministry as it emerged in the early Church. The natural bond between pastor and flock was inevitably weakened by the success of the Christian mission, because local churches grew so large that - at least in large cities - it soon became impossible for the bishop to know all his people personally. It became common to give one (or in Rome two) presbyters responsibility for each suburban or rural parish. This was division of labour for practical reasons of what was otherwise, in all but the unitary oversight which the bishop retained, an identical ministry of bishop and priest. The bishop ordained his priests for their office and confirmed those they had not themselves baptised in the parishes.

---

[22] Cf. 1922 Doctrine Commission, p. 123.

[23] See Chadwick, *op. cit.*

Bishops and presbyters belong in the New Testament to what is fundamentally a single order of ministerial priesthood. Jerome thought it so.[24] Bede emphasises that there is a common *officium*[25] and his thinking was followed by Paul the Deacon (d. 799), Rabanus Maurus and Haymo of Auxerre among the Carolingians of the next generations, and by mediaeval authors after them. The 1557 *Institution of a Christian Man* continues the tradition. It is cited in the nineteenth century by William Goode, as speaking of 'the parity of bishops and presbyters with respect to the ministerial power essentially and by right belonging to them', and he argues that in 1540 Cranmer, Bonner, Barlow, Cox, Redmayne and Edgeworth agreed that 'bishops and priests were, properly speaking, of the same order'.[26] A little later than the *Institution* Archbishop Whitgift speaks of 'an equality' of bishops and priests *quoad ministerium*, 'in their ministry'.[27] The difference we have seen emerging perhaps as early as the New Testament and increasingly clear in the post-apostolic Church is that within a single eucharistic community the priest has, pastorally speaking, an authority only as a deputy, deriving from his bishop, who is its head. In the authoritative proclamation of the Word and ministry of the sacraments the bishop is consistently seen as the chief minister throughout those communities which have kept to a threefold ministry. From his presidency of the community proceeds a responsibility for what Whitgift calls 'order and government',[28] and because the priest is his deputy, the priestly office is dependent on the episcopal through ordination.

The distinction of order which grew up between bishop and priest thus represented a much less fundamental distinction than that which is hinted at in Acts 6.1-6, between the apostles, who were to devote themselves to prayer and the ministry of the Word, and the seven who were to 'serve tables', that is, to look after the practical affairs of the community.[29] These earliest deacons were needed primarily for administrative duties. Male deacons gradually acquired limited liturgical functions, especially of reading the Gospel, but they did not preside at the Eucharist. The establishment of Christianity as the official religion of the Roman Empire in the fourth century had momentous consequences for an understanding of the episcopal office. Bishops sometimes became important imperial officials, absorbed in a burdensome work of administration and justice. It was mainly for this

---

[24] Jerome, Letter 146.
[25] *Patrologia Latina* 94.223.
[26] Goode, *Ordination*, pp. 5-6.
[27] Whitgift, *Works* III.535-6.
[28] *Ibid.*
[29] *Deacons in the Ministry of the Church* (London, 1987), 4-6.

reason that in time deacons became senior administrative officials in the diocese, on the bishop's personal staff,[30] not infrequently succeeding to episcopal office themselves, as Gregory the Great did, having once been Deacon of Rome.

This special relationship of diaconate to *episcope* was somewhat obscured by the development of a three-tiered picture of ordained ministry, in which bishop, priest and deacon are distinguished as separate 'grades'.[31] These three grades came to be seen as corresponding with the three grades of Old Testament ministry, of high priest, priest and levite. But the Old Testament typology did not create the threefold Christian ministry. That is a structure which owes its origin to the second century Church's inheritance from the sub-apostolic generation, in which an originally two-tiered ministry of bishop-priest and deacon,[32] passed into the three-tiered ministry to meet practical needs; with the presiding bishops representing apostolicity. Further ramifications of the bishop's role as administrator became apparent in the mediaeval period, when the bishop's household tended to generate officials (chancellor, chaplains and so on), and the archdeacon often saw to the tasks which the bishop need not perform in person, such as visitations, the administration of justice in ecclesiastical courts, and appointments to certain ecclesiastical offices.

All this could work in theory and in practice only if the diocese was understood to be the fundamental normal unit of Church administration, as well as remaining in a real sense the 'local eucharistic community' even when it became too large for the Christians within it to be able to worship together regularly. That has been consistent Anglican thinking in general.[33] The Lambeth Conference of 1930 speaks of the 'territorial diocese under the jurisdiction of one bishop'.[34] It must, if this is to be a useful system, remain the case that this diocesan 'local church' has a centre and focus in a personal leader,[35] who is pastor.

---

[30] *Ibid.*, pp. 8 ff.

[31] Trallians 3, 'without which a community cannot be called a church', as Ignatius goes so far as to say

[32] Cf. Taylor, *Episcopacy Asserted*, p. 20.

[33] Although in the colonial period in America the parish was perhaps seen as the basic unit.

[34] Lambeth, 1930, p. 248; cf. Lambeth, 1968, p. 58, and Gundrum, p. 4. The present Roman Catholic *Codex Iuris Canonici* says that 'a diocese is a portion of the people of God which is entrusted for pastoral care to a bishop with the co-operation of the presbyterate, so that, adhering to its pastor, and gathered by him in the Holy Spirit through the Gospel and the Eucharist, it constitutes a particular Church, in which the one, holy, catholic and apostolic Church of Christ is truly present and operative' (369).

[35] Cf. Lambeth, 1978, p. 40 and Canon C 18 and *Codex Iuris Canonici* 129.1, cf. 134, 135, 392.2.

As Jeremy Taylor put it:

> The whole cure of the diocese is in the bishop; he cannot
> exonerate himself of it, for it is a burden of Christ's imposing, or
> it is not imposed at all; therefore this taking of presbyters into
> part of the regiment and care does not divest him of his own
> power or any part of it, nor yet ease him of his care, but that as
> he must still *episkopein*, 'visit' and 'see to' his diocese, so he hath
> authority still in all parts of his diocese ... When the bishop came
> to any place, there the *vicaria* of the presbyters did cease ... and
> he being present might do any office, because it was in his own
> charge ...; and therefore *praesente episcopo* (saith the Council of
> Carthage and St. Leo) "if the bishop be present", the presbyter
> without leave might not officiate.[36]

'The whole power of ministration both of the Word and sacraments was in
the bishop by prime authority, insomuch that they might not exercise any
ordinary ministration without licence from the bishop. They had power and
capacity by their order to preach, to minister, to offer, to reconcile, and to
baptise; they were indeed acts of order but they might not by the law of the
church exercise any of these acts without license from the bishop', that is a
matter of 'jurisdiction, and shews the superiority of the bishop over his
presbyters by the practice of Christendom'.[37] It is in this context that the
Tractarians of the nineteenth century saw the bishop as a guarantor in his
person of both orthodoxy and the validity of sacramental life,[38] although the
language of 'guarantee' is now avoided ecumenically, because it has an
unhappy history in some traditions.

Suffragan bishops remain something of an anomaly. In the early
centuries *Chorepiscopoi* ('country-bishops') were sometimes appointed as
'area bishops' in large dioceses, with the diocesan bishop retaining direct
pastoral charge of the diocesan city centre. This system (which is still in use
in Syrian and Coptic Churches in particular) amounted to something very
like the formation of a Metropolitan 'diocese' with a 'province' of
surrounding 'dioceses'. In the Middle Ages and in sixteenth century
Anglican usage an Archbishop might speak of his 'suffragans' with
reference to those bishops of his province whose 'vote' (*suffragium*) he
could count on, who are 'his bishops'.

A second mediaeval usage, countenanced by the Fourth Lateran Council
of 1215, allowed 'suffragans' to be appointed in emergency, where the
diocesan bishop was ill, or had to be away from his diocese on important

[36] Taylor, *Episcopacy Asserted*, p. 156.
[37] *Ibid.*, p. 152.
[38] See, for example, John Keble, *Sermons for Saints' Days and Holy Days* and Tracts 4, 5,
7, 12, 15, 24 of Tracts for the Times.

business. In this sense, a suffragan was a temporary provision, acting as an episcopal 'vicar'.

This kind of suffragan was an established feature of late mediaeval English life, and in 1534 the Suffragan Bishops Act provided for certain towns to become 'sees', so that suffragan bishops might have titles, but with the understanding that they were to act still as episcopal vicars for diocesans temporarily unable to discharge their functions. By the late seventeenth century the suffragan was beginning to be seen as a permanency rather than as an emergency minister. But it was not until the nineteenth century that suffragans came to be consecrated systematically in England to serve with the 'titles' provided for in 1534. The problem raised by the existence of suffragan bishops as permanent officers within a diocese is that of the challenge they pose to the rule of 'one bishop, one diocese'.[39]

The ministry of Word and sacrament

The inseparable ministry of Word and sacrament in the community is central to its life, and underlies all the principles of governance and administration which have more conspicuously to do with 'authority'. The primary commission of the missionary Church was to witness to the resurrection of the Lord. The apostles received from their glorified Lord a commission to preach the Gospel. This is the twin pole to the sacramental life which Christ instituted in his baptism and in the Last Supper. In preaching the bishop is supremely the focus of the Church's unity both structurally and mystically (for nothing is more supernatural in the life of the Church than the authentic proclamation of the Word of God). Irenaeus wrote of the bishop as minister of unity in this sense: as the one who keeps the local church in the apostolic teaching. Though he shared with Ignatius a belief that the bishop was primarily a 'eucharistic person', his conflict with the Gnostics made him realise that it was essential for the bishop, who spoke from his 'teaching chair' at the Eucharist, to have the responsibility for keeping the Church firm on its apostolic foundation in matters of faith. The Gnostics claimed that they had a secret tradition which was handed down by their teachers. Irenaeus answered that the apostolic tradition was open and public, based on the Scriptures which everyone could read or hear; and taught publicly and continuously in those churches which had been founded by the apostles. A continuous succession of bishops teaching the same faith

---

[39] See *Report* of the Archbishops' Commission on the Episcopate (1990), on the question of suffragans.

from a church's 'chair' was a guarantee of orthodox doctrine.[40] The
outward continuity of consecration was clearly seen as a sign of inward
continuity of teaching.

In early Christian art Christ himself is commonly portrayed as a Teacher.
That is also a theme of much early Christian writing, and it is a key task of
the bishop as president of the local eucharistic community to give time to
study, and to preach, so that he may be equipped to be a teacher and a
guardian of the faith.[41] At the end of the fourth century Ambrose of Milan
wrote that the first duty of bishop or priest is to learn so that he may
teach.[42] Ephesians 4.11, he points out, couples the offices of pastor and
teacher. In the East and the West alike in the patristic period we see the
bishop as homilist and theologian, expounding Scripture and putting the
faith into words for his people. In the best of such leadership - exemplified
in the West in Ambrose, Augustine, Gregory the Great - spiritual
discernment, intellectual powers and sound judgement go together. The
episcopal (and by deputing, the priestly) responsibility for the ministry of
the Word is, like the ministry of the sacraments and the ministry of
leadership, at base a community activity in which the whole congregation
participates with its minister, although it is focused in the pastoral office.[43]

The ancient principle that the bishop has a special responsibility for the
ministry of the Word and the maintenance of the community in the truth of
faith is endorsed in the sixteenth century Anglican Ordinal by the presenting
of a Bible to the new bishop with the words, 'Give heed unto reading,
exhortation and doctrine'. There is a direct link here with the bishop's early
role as leader of the single local worshipping community, which was
brought out by sixteenth century reformers as they sought to redress the late
mediaeval imbalance between the ministry of the Word and the ministry of
the sacraments. They emphasised the saving power of the Word; the
ministry of the Word is seen in its proper context as central to the ministry
of reconciliation because Scripture brings people to Christ. The rite of
ordination of a bishop in the English Alternative Service Book requires the
bishop-elect to make a promise in answer to the Archbishop's question,
'Will you be diligent in prayer, in reading Holy Scripture, and in all studies
that will deepen your faith and fit you to uphold the truth of the Gospel
against error?'

---

[40] There is no real conflict here with the practice of a *disciplina arcani*, which protected the
truth from those who, in ages of persecution, sought to make a mockery of it; and which
entrusted it in its fullness only to the faithful.

[41] Cf. both the Ordinal and the Alternative Service Book forms for the ordination of a
bishop.

[42] Ambrose, *De Officiis Ministrorum* I.iii.

[43] Aquinas insists that preaching is a special responsibility of the bishop.

Jesus instituted a practice of baptism which was adopted universally in the early Church for the once-and-for-all forgiveness of sins and the reconciliation of the believer with God through faith in Christ; and to seal the believer's membership of the community. The bishop was deemed the proper person to perform the baptism, although it was always accepted that any member of the community who was baptised might do so in case of extraordinary need. Augustine underlined that it is Christ who baptises, and so an ordained minister - or indeed a worthy minister - was not an essential requirement. The indispensable elements were the intention to baptise, and the statement that the baptism was carried out in the name of Father, Son and Holy Spirit (in whom the candidate in person, or by proxy in the case of an infant, declares his or her faith); and the use of water. Canon 9 (8) of the Council of Arles, 314, says that a candidate who asks to be admitted to the Catholic fold from, for example, the Donatist sect, must be asked whether he has been baptised in the name of the Trinity. If he answers in the affirmative, he is not rebaptised. Here the bishop as leader of the community is crucial. The candidate receives the laying on of hands, so that he may receive the Holy Spirit, and he is admitted into the community as he desires. The same principle of episcopal 'confirmation' of an existing baptism by the laying on of hands is to be found in a canon of the Council of Elvira (300-3), where the individual who has been baptised by someone else in case of 'need' is brought to the bishop.[44]

Anglican practice retains, from before the separation from Rome in the sixteenth century, the ancient distinction between baptism and confirmation. The bishop alone may confirm the candidate with the laying on of hands and the epiklesis, and admit him or her to eucharistic communion. As Jeremy Taylor puts it, 'the apostles did impose hands for the confirmation of baptised people, and this was a perpetual act of power to be succeeded to, and yet not ... executed ... by any ... presbyter'.[45] The act of confirmation does not imply that the priest who baptised the candidate left something unfinished or exceeded the bounds of his office, but is the relic of the understanding that it is the bishop who, as head of the local eucharistic community, welcomes the new member to communion on behalf of that community; and his action underlines baptism's role as a process rather than an event in the Christian life.[46] There is both a confirmation of what was done at baptism and an inauguration of a new and growing fullness of life.

[44] Taylor, *Episcopacy Asserted*, p. 27.

[45] Cf. Book of Common Prayer 'daily increase'.

[46] Ignatius, *To the Smyrnaeans*, 8. The late Gareth Bennett drafted material for the English Archbishops' Commission on the Episcopate, which is drawn on here.

The central act of Christian worship, the Eucharist, is the memorial of our reconciliation through Christ's once-and-for-all sacrifice upon the Cross, and it nourishes the Church's life for the fulfilment of its mission. It is for this reason that it has always been considered right that the minister who leads the community and is its pastor and the focus of its unity, should act focally and representatively in making possible the participation of the whole community in the celebration of the Eucharist. In presiding over the Eucharist, the second-century bishop was seen as someone whose authority had divine sanction by the charism of the Spirit within the continuous succession of the Spirit-filled community. As Ignatius of Antioch describes it, God the Father and the society of heaven are represented on earth by the bishop with his presbyters and the people.

Ignatius of Antioch, writing at a time when there would have been only one Eucharistic assembly in each city, found it easy to see the people as personified in their eucharistic minister. The bishop was not a distant celebrity making a rare visit, or an administrator running the diocese's complex affairs, but the one pastor who, Sunday by Sunday, broke the bread at the Eucharist, and it was natural to see this bishop as Christ's representative, acting *in persona Christi*. Ignatius writes, 'Where the bishop is present, there let the congregation gather, just as where Jesus Christ is, there is the Catholic Church'.[47] This period when 'a Church and a Diocese seem to have been ... coextensive and identical'[48] made the community a congregation, a physical gathering. A Church is, for Ignatius, essentially a eucharistic community.

He echoes Paul's thought in I Corinthians 10.16-17. 'The bread which we break, is it not a participation in the body of Christ? Because there is one loaf, we who are many are one body, for we all partake of the same loaf'. Paul is saying that communion in one eucharistic bread is what makes individuals one in a single community. Those who share in the body of Christ become the body of Christ. Unity is not something administrative or numerical, nor is it imposed from the outside, but formed within the community by this common sharing.

In Ignatius' thought - and this is of continuing importance in the Orthodox tradition - the bishop becomes the very image of Christ, and as Christ himself draws the believers into *koinonia* or fellowship with God and with one another, so the bishop becomes the personal focus of unity for the local church. 'Be careful, then, to observe a single Eucharist', says Ignatius, 'For there is one flesh of our Lord Jesus Christ, and one cup of his blood, and that makes us one, and one altar, just as there is one bishop along with

---

[47] R. Whately, *The Kingdom of Christ* (London, 1842) II.165, para. 20.
[48] 'Ikon'.

the presbytery, and the deacons, my fellow-slaves The picture of the bishop
as primarily the eucharistic president, with his other roles depending upon
that, is a constant theme in later patristic writings. 'The Church is the
people united ... to its shepherd. From this you should know that the bishop
is in the church and the church in the bishop', says Cyprian in the third
century..[49] In the early part of the same century, Hippolytus of Rome in his
Apostolic Tradition gives a prayer for the consecration of a bishop which
calls him a 'high priest' whose task is to 'offer the gifts of the holy
church'.[50]

A series of developments combined to obscure the full 'community'
character of eucharistic presidency in succeeding centuries. The first was a
change in liturgical patterns which meant that the priest or bishop now stood
with his back to the people and that the table was placed at the end of the
Church, thus effectively separating celebrant and community. The words of
consecration began to be said in a whisper and eventually in silence. Masses
were said by the celebrant alone on occasion (and very frequently so during
the Middle Ages), so that the celebration came to seem the action not of the
community but of the priest or bishop by himself. This (largely
inadvertent) shutting out of the people and separation from the priestly
office from its role in the community was further reinforced by the
formulation of the doctrine of transubstantiation at the end of the eleventh
century. This focused attention upon the nature of the change taking place
in the consecrated elements, almost to the exclusion of the participation of
the president and people.[51]

The contrast between a 'private' and a shared celebration seemed to the
sixteenth century reformers to be a point of substance. There has been a
great and determinative change as a result of Christ's Passion, Calvin
argues, which the priests of the late mediaeval Church had been denying. In
the Old Testament tabernacle the people stood far off, and only priests were
allowed to enter the sanctuary. Now God admits us together to his sight.[52]
The call for the use of the term 'priesthood' exclusively for the priesthood
of all believers reflected this criticism, although it was common for there to

[49] Cyprian, *Letters,* 66.8.
[50] It is interesting that the ordination prayer for a presbyter in Hippolytus does not mention
the Eucharist, but concentrates on 'government and administration'; in the fourth century
the order is reversed, with the bishop having responsibility for governance and the
presbyter being the local eucharistic minister. but from Ignatius down to Cyprian in the
third century, all thought that the office of a bishop was set in a eucharistic context.
[51] It also elevated the priest to the status of miracle worker, for he came to be thought of as
possessing a power in his private person to make Christ. In the Orthodox liturgy the use
of the *epiklesis* obviates this difficulty.
[52] CR 83.91-2; cf. *Institutes* II.vii.2 and II.xv.6.

be confusion between the notion that all Christians individually are equally priests and the patristic understanding of a corporate priesthood by participation in the one sacrifice of Christ on the Cross (of which the Eucharist is a memorial, in which the risen Lord himself, as Head of the Church, now pleads his self-offering before the Father and brings his people with him into the holy of holies).

In the West in the Middle Ages, then, the bishop ceased in any ordinary sense to be the head of a eucharistic community; he tended to leave such pastoral tasks as were associated with the running of his cathedral to an assistant bishop.[53] The concept of the eucharistic community was itself eroded by the developments which encouraged people to think of 'sacerdotal power' as exercised over the community and not within it, and to direct resentment against the ordained ministry.[54] Such habits of thought were consolidated during the Reformation at a number of points, and the bishop's role in government and jurisdiction emerged as his principal and defining one. It was as 'lords spiritual' especially that bishops continued in sixteenth century England.

In our own time there has been a return to the ancient picture of the Church as first and foremost a eucharistic community. In the years before the summoning of the Second Vatican Council, Henri de Lubac was already describing the life of grace as essentially corporate, cutting through the tendency for both sides in the debates of the Reformation to oppose an individualistic spirituality and an external authoritarianism. As the Eucharist is celebrated the Church is 'made'; the eucharistic assembly is the microcosm of the whole Church, and he who presides at the Eucharist must be the community's leader in life and mission. In this way unity wells up from within the community. It is this ecclesiology, with its return to the primitive and the patristic models, which lies at the heart of the reforms of the post-Vatican II era, and which has found expression in the agreed statements of a series of ecumenical commissions in recent decades.[55]

[53] Not, it should be noted, to be equated with today's suffragan bishop. A vestige of this practice remains in the function of the dean of a modern Anglican cathedral, who acts as its vicar, and see pp. 32-3.

[54] The sixteenth century dislike of the term *sacerdos* among reformers was not matched by a corresponding campaign against the use of the term *pontifex*, although *pontifex* is the key term in Hebrews for Christ's unique priesthood.

[55] The 'disciplinary' office of the bishop and the question of the 'power of the keys' is dealt with in the chapter on *Authority in matters of morals*.

Chapter Five

Authority linking the local and universal Church

Microcosm and Macrocosm

In acting as a personal focus of the community's worship and life, the bishop is placed in a relationship to the community which makes it possible for him to act on its behalf and with its consent, in communication with other worshipping communities. As one Anglican-Orthodox Dialogue has recently put it, this sustaining of a wider communion through leaders is naturally 'expressed in constant contact and communication between the bishops and members of different local churches through meetings in council, exchanges of letters, mutual visits and prayers for each other'.[1] Maintaining in unity by means of such sharing can be seen as the specific responsibility of those with oversight in the community because it is only through their office that whole communities can remain constantly in touch with one another throughout the Church. In this second of the planes of the Church's life which have traditionally intersected in the person of the bishop the single eucharistic gathering or 'Church in each place' is linked with the community of the whole Church.

This does not compromise but rather reinforces the completeness of each local Church. In the first generations, it is clear that each local Church was seen as having within it all the elements of the universal Church. In this 'Church in each place',[2] each celebration of the Eucharist also takes place within the Catholic Church. Christ is present in his wholeness in each local celebration and so it is 'the outward manifestation of the common faith and the Christian love which binds together all local Churches in one Catholic Church'.[3] Newman put it well:

---

[1] A-O, 13. Hospitality to travellers, exchange of letters and going to represent his own people at the ordination of the ministers of neighbouring churches are included in the list from an early date.

[2] World Council of Churches, New Delhi Statement.

[3] A-O, 13.

> Each diocese is a perfect independent Church, sufficient for itself;
> and the communion of Christians one with another, and the unity
> of them all together, lie ... in what they are and what they have in
> common.

He cites Dodwell (1641-1711) and Hickes (1642-1715) in support of the
view that:

> the Church is complete in one bishopric; a number of bishoprics
> are but reiterations of one, and add nothing to the perfection of
> the system. As there is one Bishop invisible in heaven, so there is
> but one bishop on earth; and the multitude of bishops are ... one
> and all shadows and organs of one and the same divine reality.[4]

This mystical oneness in the multiplicity of eucharistic communities has its
practical counterpart in the structure of each diocese, in line with the
principles of pastoral oversight we have been looking at. The bishop's
responsibility remains at base specific. A portion of the people of God is
entrusted to his care with the help of the presbyterate, the bishop's 'fellow-
labourers'.[5] The flock, adhering to its pastor and gathered by him in the
Holy Spirit through the Gospel and the Eucharist, constitutes what we may
call a 'particular' or local church. It is of course natural for members of a
'parish' worshipping community which meets regularly within this larger
whole to feel a loyalty to their own pastor, who will be one of the bishop's
priests. But if the concept of a single diocesan community seems remote in
modern Anglican Church life in some parts of the world, it should be
remembered that the bishop still has responsibility in canon law for giving
authority to exercise priestly ministry in his diocese; so the diocese is still
seen as in principle a single community of this sort.[6] And a visit from the
bishop is still a major and exciting event for a local parish, because he is
seen by the people as 'their' bishop.

The essential completeness of the local eucharistic community with its
bishop does not make it independent of other like communities. The
autonomy of such a community was from the first subject to, or limited by,
the mutual care that local churches have for each other, or by the leadership
given by certain prominent churches which looked back to their foundation
by one of the apostles. This last is exemplified in the Epistle of Clement of
Rome to Corinth (c.96). Clement of Rome sees the duly ordained ministry
as the embodiment of the principle that God wills order in his Church. That
means that a local church, like the one at Corinth, cannot get rid of its

---

[4] John Henry Newman, 'The Catholicity of the Anglican Church', *Essays Critical and Historical* (London, 1890), II.20, 23.

[5] Cardwell, *Synodalia* II.447, English Convocation of 1555.

[6] Canon C 8.

clergy without being obliged to satisfy other churches that those who have been deposed are unworthy of their office. Similarly, frequent contacts between churches act as a check on private idiosyncrasies in teaching. They help catholicity. So the 'synodical' idea of mutual accountability has not solely a negative purpose (of imposing a restriction on what any individual bishop or church may do), but a positive and creative role to play.

The principle of mutual care among equals was not found by the second century communities to be incompatible with giving a special place to churches of apostolic foundation. (In the West such a place was occupied by Rome, where St. Peter and St. Paul died.)[7] This tradition has implications for primacy, which we shall come to later.

The sharing of authority between bishops and their churches which all this represents was needed especially in matters of faith and in matters of discipline. We shall consider each of these too more fully in later chapters. Our immediate concern here is with the underlying structures of 'order' within this second plane of episcopal responsibility, upon which these exercises of sharing rest.

The term 'collegiality' is used, sometimes confusingly, in a variety of senses. I shall take it to have a meaning derived from the brotherhood instituted by Christ among his apostles,[8] and visibly continued among the bishops of the Church in their 'college' or brotherhood. This is a use of the term which has backing in classical usage, where *collegium* describes an enduring bond among equals. In mediaeval usage, *collegium* can refer to the bond of all the faithful.[9] That is important, because episcopal 'collegiality' must always act in the context of the universal bond of collegiality which makes all the faithful brothers and equals. The vocabulary of 'conciliarity' is very ancient, but, like 'collegiality', it does not have an agreed single sense. From the earliest times Christians met to consult together when there were differences or when decisions needed to be made. The principal difference between 'conciliarity' and 'collegiality' as they are used here is this: the first refers to the exercise of consultation in the Church on particular occasions and the second to a continuous common reflection and action, as of those who share their lives in Christ. Thus conciliarity can never be separated from collegiality. All 'councils' are episodes in a continuing collegial life. They are meetings in person of those who live in perpetual brotherly fellowship, or of bishops as their

---

7   On the issues raised by the historical position of the Roman Church, see ARCIC A I and A II.

8   Cf. Luke 6.13 and Vatican II, *Lumen Gentium*.

9   Commonly in Aquinas, *collegium ecclesiae; collegium fidelium qui sunt templum dei*.

representatives.[10] Collegiality has its own dynamics and within them there operate the special dynamics of conciliarity. In all sorts of meetings these have the effect of sharpening and concentrating and bringing to a decisive point (even if only an interim one) the processes going on all the time within the life of the Church. Councils and synods and other meetings have the task of expressing and defining and making statements, and their words stand thereafter as a point of reference in subsequent discussion. Thus one may speak of 'before' and 'after' a meeting, on the understanding that a meeting brings something about, even where it does not finally settle a question.

The history of Councils

We must go back now and see how this theology fits the history. The special ministerial responsibility for safeguarding what is taught in the churches is found at an early stage. In Paul's discourse to the presbyters of Ephesus (who are called 'bishops', Acts 20.24-8), these leaders of the Church are warned to be guardians of the true tradition against the false doctrine which threatens the very existence of the Church Christ founded. So there is clear early warrant for episcopal responsibility in guarding the faith, although that in no way implies that lay people have no responsibility to share in the maintenance of the faith. It was this protective, guarding role which came to be especially carried out by synods, in which the bishop is the sacramental representative of his local community. In the middle of the third century Cyprian, Bishop of Carthage, developed the underlying theology by speaking of the bishops as a collective body uniting the various eucharistic communities. They bring to councils the faith and experience of the local church. It is here important that the universal Church is not seen as a higher level of church organisation, but as existing already in the local churches. So they are never swallowed up in a collective identity when they meet. That seems to be a key meaning of Cyprian's dictum: 'there is one episcopate in which each individual bishop has a share; *(episcopatus unus est, cuius a singulis in solidum pars tenetur).*[11] Together, and waiting on the will of God, the bishops assembled in synod, with Christ present in their midst and the Spirit in their hearts, are seen as seeking a truth which is in

10   Bullinger, *De Conciliis* I.i (Tigur, 1561), p. 4 gives a derivation and definition of *concilium (convocatio, coetus, concio)* and equates it with 'synod' in its purpose of 'judging', 'consulting', or 'treating of' subject put before it. On the place of the laity, see E. Hill, *Ministry and Authority in the Catholic Church* (London, 1988), p. 131: 'There is no dogmatic reason why synodical government should be confined to bishops, though there is a dogmatic reason why bishops should always lead it'.

11   *On the Unity of the Catholic Church, 5.*

each mind, but greater in its fullness than any individual can grasp or express. This was not the view of a mere idealist. Cyprian had some experience of councils, and he knew that there would be insistent partisans and recalcitrant minorities. But he did not want to see parties overridden; his vision was of the patient preservation of a unity in which all could agree. Unanimity was of the essence.

The conciliar functions of bishops were somewhat in abeyance during much of the mediaeval period, partly as a result of great practical difficulties in assembling many bishops in one place in the unsettled society of the period after the fall of the Roman Empire in the West. Local councils did meet, particularly in the Carolingian period, as assemblies of the bishops of 'national' churches, and at that time there was certainly no sense in the West that this was in any sense in conflict with acceptance of a Roman primacy.[12] From the late eleventh century, vigorous assertion of papal plenitude of power[13] eclipsed Western conciliar government of the Church except for the series of Lateran Councils of the eleventh and twelfth centuries until, in the Conciliar movement of the fourteenth and fifteenth centuries, episcopal and conciliar government was set over against 'papal monarchy', and it became difficult if not impossible to see primatial and conciliar government as complementary.[14]

The sixteenth century thinkers brought a number of assumptions about the nature of conciliar government to the framing of the formularies of the Church of England. Article XXI of the Thirty-Nine Articles speaks only of General Councils. Its preoccupation is with their summoning ('General Councils may not be gathered together without the commandment and will of Princes'), with their potential for error ('they may err') and with their authority ('things ordained by them as necessary to salvation have neither strength nor authority, unless it be declared that they be taken out of Holy Scripture').[15] These concerns arose directly out of topics of heated contemporary debate among reformers, and like much else in the sixteenth century discussion of problems of authority, the debate here suffered from a tendency to divide up the issues into *theses* or 'articles' suitable for treatment in formal disputation. The same polemical preoccupations recurred again and again in the writings of the sixteenth century divines, and made it difficult for anyone to develop a positive, balanced and comprehensive conciliar theory. The first Anglicans had - and knew they

---

12 Y. Congar, *L'ecclésiologie du haut moyen âge* (Paris, 1968) gives an account of this.
13 Pope Gregory VII and Bernard of Clairvaux were the seminal figures here.
14 See B. Tierney, *Foundations of the Conciliar Theory* (Cambridge, 1955).
15 Cf. *Reformation Legum Ecclesiasticarum*, 14, ed. E. Cardwell, *Synodalia*, p. 6. On conciliar error, see Rogers, PS, pp. 209-10, Hooper, PS 1.526-7.

had - an imperfect knowledge of the early councils and later ones alike;[16] they were aware that they were working with faulty texts.[17] But they thought they had stressed the key points.

In the circumstances of the time it was of importance for the Anglican reformers to stress the normality of a secular sovereign summoning a council and ratifying its decrees. It was argued that, apart from the councils of the primitive Church, this had historically been the pattern.[18] In any case, it was protested, a council called by a Pope could not be 'free'.[19] The bishops who came to it will be the Pope's men and must vote as he directs.[20]

The membership of councils was also widely discussed. Three points commonly arose here: whether it is important that the council should consist of 'good men';[21] whether a larger number carries more weight than a smaller number; whether a council must be 'representative' of the whole Church. These last two points are interrelated. Latimer says that a larger number is not necessarily better; it is not a matter of a majority decision.[22] There was some awareness here of a patristic sense that a council should have the widest possible base, but apparently no strong feeling in favour of the universality for which Cyprian and Celestine I had pressed.[23] 'Representativeness' is a much more complex matter in sixteenth century eyes, and we shall return to its implications when we come to the question of the forming of a common mind in matters of faith. Ignatius had argued at the turn of the first century that the whole Church entrusted to a bishop is present in his person.[24] This sense seems less strong in the sixteenth century debates. Indeed Luther reviles the whole idea of representativeness.[25]

Priests as bishops' deputies in councils and synods had an established English history. By 1283 the Convocation of Canterbury included abbots and deans and archdeacons, with two representatives from the clergy of each diocese; and by the fifteenth century the bishops and clergy sat as two

---

16 Greenslade, art. *cit.*, 96-7.
17 Jewel, *Works*, PS I.341.
18 Rogers, PS 205.
19 Greenslade, art. *cit.*, pp. 101, 104, 106.
20 Jewel, PS 3.205.
21 Latimer, PS 1.288. (But Cranmer says that error is still possible, PS 2.53.)
22 Latimer, PS 1.288; cf. Greenslade, p. 101.
23 Henry Chadwick, 'The status of ecumenical councils in Anglican Thought', *Orientalia Christiana Analecta* 195 (1973), 393, cites Cyprian, Ep. 55.6, a letter written to Rome to ask whether their consensus can be added to that of the oriental bishops. Pope Celestine is cited (p. 394), Ep. 18.1, PL 50.506A and citing Matthew 18.20, a letter written to the Council of Ephesus, 431.
24 *Ibid.*, p. 393, citing Ignatius, *Ad Eph.* 1, *Ad Magn.* 2, *Ad Trall.* 1.
25 E.g. Weimar Ausgabe 39^i.192-3.

Houses. The English model was preserved after the Reformation and deliberately matched in the sixteenth century to the structure of Lords and Commons in Parliament. Edmund Grindal, as Archbishop of Canterbury, wanted to strip bishops of their autocratic character and stress presbyteral assistance, but he died in 1583 with his reforms uncompleted. In the late eighteenth century and the early nineteenth century a long wrangle took place between upper and lower Houses of Convocation in an endeavour to settle the question of the clergy's right to initiate and conclude business, over against that of the bishops.[26] In 1717 the Convocations were prorogued by the Crown and they did not meet again for over a century. The further question whether a council can be representative of the whole community unless it consists of bishops, clergy and laity[27] did not become a burning issue among Anglicans until the nineteenth century. We shall come to that too in due course.

At issue in all this in the sixteenth century debates was whether a council's decrees could have any force at all if it was not properly summoned, or its work not properly ratified, or its membership in some way lacking. The question of the guidance of the Holy Spirit was raised, but the notion of Christ's presence where two or three are gathered in his name, and the concomitant principle that Christ must be the president of any true council seemed more important[28] against the background of revolt against 'papalism'. Here the reformers' concern was to prevent any usurpation of Christ's Headship of the Church. The suspicion was that a council was liable to be a 'human' institution and, without divine guidance, to behave as though its decrees could add to Scripture or even outweigh or contradict its teaching.

It was for this reason that there was so much talk of 'error' in conciliar decisions,[29] and so much underlining of the importance of consonance with Scripture as the test of all conciliar decrees. It seemed obvious to those who framed the Thirty-Nine Articles that some Councils have erred; that their definitions even sometimes contradict one another. They argued that that must mean that no-one's faith is 'bound' by a council unless what it has said can be confirmed out of Scripture.[30] Councils cannot make a rule of faith, says Jewel.[31] Tyndale, Cranmer, Whitaker, and a host of others agree that

---

[26] Lathbury, p. 468 ff.

[27] E.g. Whitaker, PS 22 and 415 and Fulke, PS 1.253; Jewel, PS 3.205.

[28] E.g. Jewel, PS 2.995.

[29] See for example Chadwick, 'The status', p. 395.

[30] *Ibid.*, p. 401 and Cardwell, p. 6.

[31] Jewel, PS 2.996.

Scripture is the guide and judge of all that councils do.[32] But even if there
was some suspicion in England of the record of councils, the principle of
equality of episcopal brotherhood in guardianship of the faith was affirmed
by the sixteenth century settlement.[33] In his Conference with Fisher,
Archbishop Laud in the seventeenth century set out a case for the view that
'the Church being as large as the world, Christ thought it fitter to govern it
aristocratically', that is, by a multiple episcopate. 'I have carefully
examined this for the first six hundred years,' he says, 'even to within the
time of S. Gregory the Great.'[34] As Laud saw it, it is the duty of bishops to
provide a system of checks and balances in mutual correction. What was
done amiss by a bishop, he says, was corrigible by a synod of bishops.[35]
Thus, as Newman was later to put it, 'bishops everywhere ... are the
elementary centures of unity', and bishop is superior to bishop only in rank
(for example, as archbishop or metropolitan, not as having superior
authority episcopally).[36]

In 1606, Richard Field published a treatise *Of the Church*, in which he
reflected at some length on the purposes councils served when something
went wrong with the normal system of checks and balances. General
Councils, he thought, were called for three reasons, 'the suppressing of new
heresies, formerly not condemned'; 'a general and uniform reformation of
abuses crept into the Church'; and 'the taking away of schisms grown into
patriarchal Churches, about the election of their pastors'.[37] About these
aspects of emergency decision-making in a conciliar framework we shall
have more to say later (see Chapter 8). Field was also interested in
representativeness. He comments that those with 'authority to teach, define,
prescribe, and to direct' have the 'deciding and defining voices', but that
laymen may be present, too, 'to hear, set forward, and consent unto that
which is there to be done'.[38] He insists upon the importance of openness.
There must be no 'secret' meeting[39] (a point with which the Dean of
Westminster agreed in 1867, and which he criticised in the conduct of the
first Lambeth Conference). Field thought that 'patriarchs' ought to preside
in councils 'as having an honourable pre-eminence above and before other

---

[32] Tyndale, PS 3.99; Becon, PS 391-2; Cranmer, PS 2.36; Rogers, PS 210. For a more
      recent bibliography than that available in Tierney, see B. Gogan, *The Common Corps
      of Christendom* (Leiden, 1982).

[33] Cf. *Articuli Cleri*, 1558, v, Cardwell, *Synodalia* II.493.

[34] Laud, *Works*, 2.222.

[35] Laud, Conference with Fisher IX.ix.26, p. 224.

[36] Newman, 'The Catholicity', pp. 24, 29.

[37] Richard Field, *Of the Church* (Cambridge, 1854), IV.3 (Book V.48).

[38] *Ibid.*, V.49, p. 15.

[39] *Ibid.*

bishops, in such assemblies'.[40] He believed that the Holy Spirit did not guide councils in such a way that they were guaranteed to be free from error. That is clear from the fact that they proceed by 'meditation, study and research' and do not expect 'immediate revelation'.[41] There are hints here of the picture of a central and pivotal, but qualified and limited role for bishops in conciliar government. Yet the sixteenth century preoccupations are still dominant and the concept of Lambeth 1988 of each bishop 'bringing his diocese with him' is not quite squarely in frame in Field's account.

William Laud's Conference with Fisher the Jesuit in 1622 represents a new[42] departure because Laud gave serious thought to the question of the powers of independent action of provincial or national synods representing only part of the universal Church. 'The making of canons, which must bind all particular Christians and Churches, cannot be concluded and established', he said, except in a General Council. When a situation arises - as it had done in the sixteenth century, when there is an emergency with which only a General Council can deal, but it is not possible to hold one,[43] the Church must pray for such a Council and either wait for it, 'or else reform itself *per partes*, by means of national or provincial synods'. He says that that is not an idea which ought to surprise us;[44] it is 'as lawful for a particular Church' ... 'to reform what is amiss in doctrine or manners' as it is for it to 'publish or promulgate' the catholic faith.[45] It is surely better to do that than to wait?[46] He cites Jean Gerson (1363-1429) as his authority for saying that a Church may be reformed *per partes*.[47] This is not envisaged by Laud as a licence for independent local action in everything, but as an emergency measure only.

In the middle years of the nineteenth century Lathbury looked back over the history of councils and synods in the English Church. He has found, he says, that both laity and clergy are profoundly ignorant of the history and proceedings of Convocation, and therefore unable to take a sensible view of the case for reviving it.[48] Anglicans had lost touch with their heritage of conciliar government since Convocation had ceased to meet. Lathbury set out to show, in his *History of the Convocation of the Church of England*

---

[40]   *Ibid.*, V.20, pp. 16-7.
[41]   *Ibid.*, V.51, p. 48.
[42]   Dvornik, art. *cit.*
[43]   A debate on the holding of a General Council went through several stages among the Lutherans and caught the imagination of sixteenth century Anglican divines.
[44]   Laud, *Works* (Oxford, 1849) 2.235 (XXVI.14).
[45]   *Ibid.*, pp. 167-8 (XXIV.1-2).
[46]   *Ibid.*, p. 169 (XXIV.2).
[47]   *Ibid.*, p. 170; Jean Gerson, *De Concilio Generali*, 1.
[48]   Lathbury, p. iv of second ed., Preface to first edition.

'that the Anglican Church had her diocesan, provincial and national synods, from a very early period'. He underlined her 'independence';[49] and in the chapters which cover the centuries from 596-1532 gave accounts only of English synods and no picture at all of developments in conciliar theory in the wider Church during the Middle Ages.

This chauvinism leads him to gloss over precisely the problems which were to be of central importance in the 1860s when the question of provincial autonomy arose. He knows that some raise difficulties about the revival of Convocation, saying that an English Convocation could not meet the needs of the Irish Church, or of the 'colonial' dioceses. But 'surely', he says, 'the Church of Ireland may act for itself, and meet in its own convocation', and 'it will be easy for Convocation to devise measures' to meet the needs of the colonial dioceses. 'As it is competent for convocation to advise the Crown in the establishment of bishoprics in our colonies, so would it be equally within their province to submit to her majesty some place for synodical action in all distant dioceses'; besides: 'the colonial Churches will never desire independence as long as the colonies depend on the British Crown'.[50] He was getting into deeper water here than he could have known, both because he was not able in the circumstances of the day to see how rapidly it would cease to be the case that the British Crown could exercise any sort of royal supremacy throughout the Anglican Communion; and because he had not thought the theology through very far in the context of its implications for the universal Church.

The Lambeth Conference

In 1863 John Colenso, Bishop of Natal, appealed to the British Privy Council against a judgement of his own Archbishop deposing him for his opinions.[51] The case raised a principle of provincial jurisdiction with such ramifications that it prompted the Canadian bishops to declare themselves 'disturbed by recent declarations in high places in our Motherland, in reference to the Colonial Branches of the Mother Church'.[52] They regarded recent events as 'tending to shake the conviction, always so dear to us, that we in the Colonies were, in all respects, *one with* the Church of our parent country'.[53] They proposed as a means of ensuring that decisions affecting

[49]   *Ibid.*, p. 10.
[50]   *Ibid.*, p. 530.
[51]   See *Historical Records of the Province of South Africa*, ed. C. Lewis and G.E. Edwards (1934), pp. 310-56.
[52]   Printed in R.T. Davidson, *Origin and History of the Lambeth Conferences, 1867 and 1878* (London, 1888), p. 32.
[53]   *Ibid.*

provinces of the whole Communion were not made in the English Convocation, without the participation of those they would subsequently touch, that there should be a 'National Synod of the bishops of the Anglican Church at home and abroad'.[54] This they saw as a 'means ... by which the members of our Anglican Communion in all quarters of the world should have a share in the deliberations for her welfare, and be permitted to have a representation in one General Council of her members gathered from every land'.[55] The enterprise was conceived by the Canadians at this stage as essentially conciliar, indeed as the next best thing to 'the assembling of a General Council of the whole Catholic Church', which they recognise to be 'at present impractical'.[56] This was the first serious Anglican test of the principles of an episcopal system in which the bishop's office was to act as officer on behalf of his local community in maintaining unity in the wider Church, and it required some rethinking of what constitutes a Church an entity in a nation or region.

The Canadian proposal was taken seriously and discussed in both the Lower and the Upper Houses of Convocation in England. There, strong prejudices emerged on the subject of councils, and both clergy and bishops expressed views much coloured by the concerns of sixteenth century and subsequent Anglican theology. Dr. Jebb saw Councils as an 'emergency' provision, for 'a temporary consultation between the different branches of Christ's Church'. They make, he thought, 'an appeal to the law of God, to the universal belief of the Christian Church'. Their function is not to argue, or even to 'reason' upon 'subjects of dispute', but to enable those who hold 'the divine authority of the Church' to 'say what is the faith of the Church from the beginning'. The bishops in a council thus 'maintain to the end' that given faith. As he sees it they do not act as 'representatives' of the people of God in this, but as those having a responsibility of guardianship.[57] Canon Hawkins thought the function of bishops meeting 'face to face in common council' was a simpler matter: 'to bring them to a better understanding of the common wants of the Church', and 'to give them heart and courage to undertake their several duties'.[58] The Dean of Westminster argued that Councils had had a place in the early centuries, but that their history since had not been encouraging. 'The general course of their steps has been marked by crime and sin.'[59] Canon Seymour was concerned over the

---

54   *Ibid.*, pp. 34-5.
55   *Ibid.*, p. 33.
56   *Ibid.*, p. 34.
57   *The Chronicle of Convocation*, Feb. 13, 1867, p. 724.
58   *Ibid.*, p. 34.
59   *Ibid.*, pp. 731-2, cf. Chadwick, 'The status', p. 397 on this point.

question of 'bindingness'. 'I understood,' he said, that 'it was a received axiom in the Catholic Church that ... articles of faith were not binding upon the whole Church until the Church had received them ... laymen giving their assent in the ancient church'.[60] Recourse was had to the deliberations of the Convocation of Canterbury in 1536,[61] and to sixteenth century references to Gregory Nazianzen's dislike of councils.[62] But this attempt to find sixteenth century precedent for opposing the calling of an Anglican Council was countered by the Rev. J.W. Joyce. 'I think ... that Gregory Nazianzen was not always opposed to synods. He had his mind changed, and so we may hope other minds ... may change also'. He cited Gregory's 'heavenly vision' of himself 'sitting on his throne, with his Presbyters around him and his Deacons before him, dealing with great questions of heavenly truth'. He himself had a vision that 'the result of this meeting of all the bishops in communion with us may be that we shall unite, first with the Greek Church, and afterwards with other Churches'.[63]

It is worth dwelling at some length on these debates, because they show how inchoate in some respects was Anglican conciliar theory at this crucial stage in the forming of practical policies for the conciliar or synodical administration and government of the growing Communion. That is not to say that there was a lack of sophistication, or of knowledge of precedents and historical background. But knowledge was clearly patchy, and it is evident that circumstances had not yet forced development of a balanced and considered doctrinal position.

The chief anxieties focused at this point on three topics: the question of the role of the laity; Royal Supremacy; and implications concerning Roman Catholic relations. All three were touched on by Canon Blakesley in the debate of February 13th, 1867. 'I am perfectly sure,' he said, that 'the English laity would not think themselves sufficiently represented by the Bishops of this Church'.[64] Nor does he think such an assembly could be brought together without the permission of the Crown.[65] And he is against councils on the grounds that they give an appearance of a final decision having been made. 'A wrong authoritative decision,' he says, then has to be explained 'by some fresh theory, which in its turn requires new glosses of authority to explain it'. This he sees as the 'Roman' way.[66] He himself sees

---

60   *Ibid.*, p. 778, Feb. 14.
61   *Ibid.*, p. 789.
62   Cf. Cranmer, PS 2.464 and Jewel, PS 4.908.
63   *The Chronicle of Convocation*, Feb. 14, 1867, pp. 768-9.
64   *Ibid.*, p. 719.
65   *Ibid.*
66   *Ibid.*, p. 720 and cf. 715.

no need for a council. In his opinion those matters which it would be proper and helpful for any such assembly to discuss might be settled by 'a few intelligent, sincere, and pious men, having the confidence of their several Churches, with the ocean penny post and a little correspondence'.[67]

This proposal to substitute a postal committee of reliable individuals for a meeting of bishops touches on the heart of the principle of a special episcopal responsibility for maintaining unity among local churches, and also upon the question of what is and what is not a council. The Dean of Westminster drew attention to the latter point as a concern which underlay all three of the pervasive anxieties in the debate. He pointed out that the Convocation of Canterbury in 1536 had said that it would be necessary to consider not only who had the authority to call together a General Council, and the order of proceeding it should follow, and whether it was really needed, but who ought to be 'judges' in it, and 'what doctrines are to be allowed or defended'.[68] The question of the 'bindingness' of any such assembly and its right to open up questions of faith, preoccupied the Upper House in its own debates. Several speakers drew back from the possibility of convening anything which could properly be called a Council.[69] 'That which is not a council of the Church cannot pretend to do that which it belongs to a council to do - i.e. to lay down any declaration of faith,' said the Bishop of Oxford. 'Such declarations are binding when laid down by a properly constituted council or Synod, he thinks, 'because such bodies have a right to claim the inspiration and over-ruling presence of him who guides the Church to a right decision. I do not believe that any body but a council, claiming to act as a council, can look for the fulfilment of those promises which are made to the Church'.[70]

Questions about 'bindingness' and inerrancy were being raised here which we must consider more fully later. But there was clearly a sense that a meeting labelled a 'council' would raise certain expectations and present difficulties of conscience for some who had reservations either about the general question of the possibility that councils may err, or about the powers of a council of bishops of Anglican Churches to 'bind' the members of the Communion. Archbishop Longley was anxious to reassure on both counts. He told the Upper House that at the meeting to be summoned in response to the Canadian bishops' request 'no declaration of faith shall be made, and no decision come to that shall affect generally the interests of the Church'. The meeting should be for 'brotherly counsel and

---

[67] *Ibid.*, p. 720.
[68] *Ibid.*, p. 789.
[69] *Ibid.*, p. 806-7.
[70] *Ibid.*, p. 804.

encouragement'.[71]   Thus the question of lay participation and
'representativeness' need not arise; there was no difficulty about summoning
a 'council' without royal initiative or consent, with the complications of its
involving, for example, bishops from America where the royal writ did not
run; and there was no danger of running into the difficulties into which
'Roman councils' were felt to have got the Church in the West in the Middle
Ages and the Roman Catholic Church since Trent. The principle was stated
more fully in the Archbishop's opening address to the Conference which
eventually met at Lambeth in 1867. 'It has never been contemplated that we
should assume the functions of a general synod of all the churches in full
communion with the Church of England, and take upon ourselves to enact
canons that should be binding upon those here represented. We merely
propose to discuss matters of practical interest and pronounce what we deem
expedient in resolutions which may serve as safe guides to future action'.
He noted that 'We have no distinct precedent to direct us'. This experiment
was seen as something new in Anglican - and indeed in Christian -
conciliarity.[72] So the Lambeth meetings came to be known as 'Conferences'
and they remain conscious that they can make no decision binding on the
member Churches of the Communion.

But something more was needed by way of clarification of the authority
of structures involving the bishops in collective responsibilities whether
collegial, conciliar, or of some other kind. The Canadian request had been
made because the South African case raised in an acute and urgent form the
question of jurisdiction. The Lambeth Conference met in recognition that
even the assembled bishops of the Anglican Communion (and it should be
remembered that not all were willing to come, and that there remained
some suspicion of the project), could not collectively enact decisions of even
the most modest sort binding on provinces which had their own legislative
structures and procedures. The theme was of such importance in the minds
of some at least of those who came that a party (the Bishop of Capetown
prominent among them) succeeded in getting the programme changed. The
second day of the meeting of 1867 was spent in discussing the due gradation
of synodical, diocesan, provincial and 'patriarchal' authority in the Anglican
Communion. A Resolution was made in favour of the 'due and canonical
subordination of the synods of the several branches to the higher authority

71   *Ibid.*, p. 807 and Davidson, p. 7.
72   Davidson, p. 10.

of a synod or synods above them'.[73] A Committee was appointed to look into 'the regulations and function of ... Synods'.[74]

The Greek root which gives us 'synod' is strictly interchangeable with the Latin-derived 'council', but the type of 'synod' the Committee describes is of a specific sort, a regular (as distinct from occasional or emergency) meeting of a constitutional body of three 'houses' of bishops, clergy and laity, at diocesan, or provincial level. For certain purposes such a synod replaces the 'convocation', a term used of assemblies of bishops and clergy since at least the seventh century in England. Historically, as we have seen, although councils have always been meetings of bishops, they have not always included clergy, and rather rarely lay people.[75]

The Committee Report of 1867 sets out the principles on which Anglican synodical government has since come to depend. It takes the diocesan Synod as 'the primary' as well as the 'simplest form of such organisation'. In such a synod, it says, the 'representation' question is met by having lay and clerical members, and the force of its decisions rests on co-operation and consent. That is to say, it is a means by which 'the co-operation of all members of the body is obtained in Church action', and 'that acceptance of Church rules is secured, which, in the absence of other law, usage, or enactment, gives to these rules the force of laws "binding on those who, expressly or by implication, have consented to them".'[76] This was not seen as an innovation. 'It is not at variance with the ancient principles of the Church, that both Clergy and Laity should attend the diocesan Synod ... it is expedient that the Synod should consist of the Bishop and Clergy of the Diocese, with Representatives of the Laity'.[77] A 'voting' laity is of course a different matter from an 'attending' laity; and the Committee does not go into the concept of a representativeness by 'classes' in the Church (that is to say, a system which makes lay people represent the laity rather than bishops representing the whole people of God in their local church).

It is a pity that more was not made of these points in the 1867 Committee Report because the result is a structural untidiness which may seem an inequity in the provision for lay representation. Strictly, the *laos* is the whole people of God; those who are ordained are lay people too. When we speak of 'lay participation' we normally, but improperly, mean the participation of those who are not ordained. In the synodical structure the

[73] Davidson, pp. 12, 48.

[74] *The Five Lambeth Conferences*, ed. R.T. Davidson (London, 1920), Report of the Committee appointed to look into 'the relations and functions of ... Synods' (1867), p. 58.

[75] Cf. Codex Iuris Canonici, 440.

[76] *The Five Lambeth Conferences*, p. 58.

[77] Lambeth, 1867, p. 58; cf. 1930, p. 250.

laos is divided into classes or 'houses' in manner which created an artificial class of 'laity' from those who are not bishops or clergy. That does not ease the problem of anticlericism. And it obscures the real implications of such recommendations as that of the Resolution of the 1968 Conference that 'no major issue in the life of the Church should be decided without the full participation of the laity in discussion and decision'.[78]

Again we must leave a fuller consideration of all this to the chapter on decision-making in matters of faith. Our immediate concern is with 'order' and structural provisions. The 1867 document goes on to discuss procedure. The principle of episcopal oversight is secure. The bishop presides in the diocesan synod. But 'the concurrent assent of Bishop, Clergy and Laity should be necessary to the validity of all acts of the Synod'. Where it is requested 'votes should be taken by orders'. Normally the Synod should meet in a 'fixed and periodical way', but the 'right of convening special meetings is retained by the bishop, so that the Synod may serve as as emergency council to meet special need.[79] Below diocesan level there have been various provisions for lay participation in deanery synods and parochial church councils and so on.[80]

We come now to an Anglican structural pattern which seems on the face of it to challenge the principle that the diocese is the fundamental and natural unit, but which in fact enacts the higher rule of collegiality and conciliarity. The 1978 Lambeth Conference, like earlier ones, urges that 'those Dioceses which still remain isolated should, as circumstances may allow, associate themselves into a Province or Provinces'. There are two reasons given for such association. It is 'in accordance with the ancient laws and usages of the Catholic Church'.[81] And history shows an evolution from an oversight focused in the bishop as president of the eucharist community to the coming together of bishops in council at a regional level.[82] It is a means of that 'sufficient and effective organisation' of the several parts of the Church 'which tends to promote the unity of the whole'.[83] It 'gives

---

78   Lambeth, 1968, p. 37. Whitgift reflected in some uncertainty upon a mediaeval tradition which envisaged the laity as a humbler and lowlier class of Christian of whom less was required by God, and who could not be expected to make a useful practical contribution to the Church's authorising. 'The inequality of ... persons, and great difference betwixt them both in godliness, zeal, learning, experience and age ... ought to be well considered' (Whitgift, Cartwright, p. 29 ff.).

79   Lambeth, 1867, p. 59.

80   See Nuttall and Pobee in Sykes on synodical government in other provinces of the Anglican Communion.

81   Lambeth, 1978, p. 84.

82   Resp., 220.

83   Lambeth, 1978, p. 84.

practical expression to the Church's fundamental principle of fellowship', facilitating 'consultation' and 'common action' and helping to keep the dioceses in mind of their 'proper relationship to the whole Church'.[84] In short, it is seen as the first step towards embodying in a structural unity the baptismal unity of the whole body of Christ on earth, and that is why we may speak of a 'higher rule' here.

The 1867 Lambeth Conference envisaged the constitution and running of provincial synods as identical in general shape to that of diocesan synods, with the difference that a house of bishops led by an archbishop takes the place of a single bishop. It was seen as the historical norm that bishops should come together on a regular basis in councils at regional level[85] and the Lambeth Conference of 1930 endorses the view that 'the minimum organisation essential to provincial life is a House or College of Bishops which can act corporately' in discharging its 'responsibility for guarding the faith, order and discipline of the Church'.[86] But the 1920 Conference had already stressed that 'a newly constituted synod of Bishops' ought to 'proceed as soon as possible to associate with itself in some official way the clergy and laity of the Province'.[87] The principle here is that although there is a clear 'collegial responsibility of the episcopate', 'synodical government' (in the sense we have been describing, involving laity and clergy as well as bishops) should go with it, to 'make provision for this responsibility to be fulfilled',[88] in a manner which makes it more fully collegial, as including the whole *collegium* of the faithful.

The diocesan synods stand in a relationship of mutual authentication to provincial synods. That is to say, the provincial synod is formed by 'voluntary association of dioceses for united legislation and common action', but at the same time, the constitution of the diocesan synod is fixed or sanctioned by the provincial synod. The diocese, in the opinion of the 1867 Committee, is 'bound to accept positive enactments of a Provincial Synod in which it is duly represented, and ... no Diocesan regulations have force, if contrary to the decisions of a higher Synod'. The Provincial Synod is thus, legislatively and morally, able to deal with 'questions of common interest to the whole Province'.[89] The Provincial Synod exercises, within the limits of

---

84 Lambeth, 1930, p. 249.

85 Resp., 220. See Wilberforce, *Inquiry*, p. 74 ff. on the principle that the unity of the episcopate is a condition of its existence and the episcopate is a trust held by all bishops in common.

86 Lambeth, 1930, pp. 249-50, cf. *Codex Iuris Canonici* 431, 433, 434, 440, 441, 442, 447, 451, 453.

87 Lambeth, 1920, Resolution 43, p. 46.

88 Lambeth, 1978, p. 76.

89 *The Five Lambeth Conferences*, pp. 59-60.

the province,[90] powers in regard to provincial questions similar to those
which the diocesan synod exercises, within the diocese, in regard to diocesan
questions. 'The spheres of action of the several Synods should be defined on
the following principle, viz., That the Provincial Synod should deal with
questions of common interest to the whole Province, and with those which
affect the Communion of the Dioceses with one another and with the rest of
the Church; whilst the Diocesan Synod should be left free to dispose of
matters of local interest and to manage the affairs of the Diocese'. The
principle of 'subsidiarity' (nothing should be done at a higher level than is
necessary) clearly underlies this practical ruling and preserves the diocesan
synod as the fundamental unit of Church organisation in such a conciliar
structure.[91]

As we move beyond the relationship of diocesan to provincial Church
government into the sphere of 'higher authority' we begin to encounter
questions which in present circumstances place a great strain on the
principle that the bishop is the officer through whom local and universal are
held together in the Church's life. The issue of 'provincial autonomy' arises
in the Anglican Communion, together with the question of the relationship
of primacy to conciliarity, and the special difficulties of maintaining
universality in a divided Church.

Instruments of higher authority

Anglican experience has been that all attempts so far to create a higher body
of a synodical sort in which the provinces of the whole Communion might
meet have proved unacceptable. As we saw in the debates before and in the
early years of the Lambeth Conferences, this has been both a cause and the
effect of difficulties about provincial autonomy. In practice, the dioceses
which make up a province have as a rule had a sufficient sense of fellowship
and common interest to make it possible for individual dioceses to submit to
combined decisions with a sense of contributing fully to the authorising
involved. The local bonds of language and culture and economy, and of
relationship with secular government, have strengthened ties within
provinces. But such bonds do not necessarily exist between provinces in the

---

90   Lambeth, 1867, p. 60. In England as the State 'became impartial in religion' (Church
     and State, p. 14, Para. 43), the Convocation of Canterbury resumed debate (1852) and
     the Convocation of York in 1861. A House of Laity was attached to the Canterbury
     Convocation in 1885, and to the Convocation of York in 1892.

91   Cf. Lambeth, 1867, p. 59, 'The constitution of the Diocesan Synod may be determined
     either by rules for that branch of the Church established by the Synod of the Province,
     or by general consent in the Diocese itself, its rules being sanctioned afterwards by the
     Provincial Synod'.

same way, and differences of a cultural and regional sort have proved to be an important source of that fear that identity is threatened which prompts the assertion of independence. The 1867 Committee which outlined an Anglican theory of synodical government saw the provincial synod as acting as a link 'securing unity' not only among its constituent dioceses, but also between these dioceses and 'other Churches of the Anglican Communion'.[92] It is to deal both with questions of common interest to the whole Province and also with the rest of the Church'.[93] But the Committee was aware of the practical obstacles to going further and attempting to make a meeting of a higher synod enact canons binding upon the whole Communion in the same way that those of a provincial synod were binding on its dioceses. 'The objection that may be urged against the united action of Churches which are more or less free to act independently [of the state], and other Churches whose constitution is fixed, not only by ancient ecclesiastical laws and usages, but by the law of the State, are obvious'. 'Under present circumstances ... no Assembly that might be convened would be competent to enact canons of binding ecclesiastical authority on these different bodies'.[94] The difficulty, in other words, was in part legislative and constitutional, and belonged to the same realm of concern as that expressed in the Lower House of the English Convocation about the need for the Crown to convene anything which wished to call itself a council. No enactment of such a body could be legally binding everywhere in the Anglican Communion. Its decisions could only 'possess the authority which might be derived from the moral weight of such united counsels and judgements, and from the voluntary acceptance of its conclusions by any of the Churches there represented'.[95]

---

[92]   *The Five Lambeth Conferences*, p. 60.

[93]   *Ibid.* and p. 61.

[94]   *Ibid.*, p. 62 and Emmaeus, p. 10. The respect of Lambeth 1867 for local custom reappears in 1878 in the provision that the 'duly-certified action of every ... particular Church, and of each ecclesiastical Province, in the exercise of its own discipline, should be respected by all the other Churches, and by their individual members' (p. 84). The Conference of 1888 thought that this rule was being neglected (p. 149). In the discussion of Lambeth 1930, we find a respect for the need to represent the 'Christian religion and the Catholic Faith in a manner congenial to the people of the land, and to give scope to their genius in the development of Christian life and worship' (p. 155). In the legislative arena, the 1867 Conference refers to the difficulty of 'united action' by Churches 'which are more or less free to act independently, and other Churches whose constitution is fixed, not only by ancient ecclesiastical laws and usages, but by the law of the State' (p. 61). 'No assembly that might be convened would be competent to enact canons of binding ecclesiastical authority to these different bodies' (p. 62).

[95]   *The Five Lambeth Conferences*, p. 62.

But there remains a deeper reason of an ecclesiological kind, which is hinted at in the vocabulary used by the Lambeth Conferences in discussing the question. The 1920 Conference quoted the Encyclical Letter of 1908. 'Regard must be had to the just freedom of 'the several parts' of the Anglican Communion, and 'the just claims of the whole communion upon its every part'.[96] The Conference of 1930 saw Anglican ecclesiastical organisation as 'regional autonomy within one fellowship'.[97] The question is whether and in what sense the provincial ecclesial bodies are 'Churches' as well as 'churches', that is, something more than local communities within an Anglican Church. Talk of 'interdependence', as well as of 'independence' implies that they are Churches, as does the habit of speaking of an 'Anglican Communion' rather than of an 'Anglican Church'.

There have been several explorations of the type of organ or organs of higher authority which might work in such a Communion.[98] The 1888 Lambeth Conference explored the possibility of the 'formation of a central Council of Reference, to which recourse may be had for advice on questions of doctrine and discipline by the tribunals of appeal of the various Provinces of the Anglican Communion'.[99] The plan foundered and did not appear in the Resolutions of 1897. But in 1908 we find the view expressed that the twofold process of expansion and consolidation which has been going on in the Anglican Communion points to the necessity for some form of central consultative body to supply information and advice. It was envisaged that this must win 'moral authority' by proving itself useful.[100] A Central Consultative Council had been formed and had met in 1901, on an experimental basis, but it stopped short of being in any sense a Tribunal of Reference with teeth, mainly because the problem of jurisdiction could not be overcome.[101] The 1948 Conference concluded that it was 'unwisely' that former Lambeth Conferences had rejected attempts to give the Conference the status of a legislative synod; or proposals for an Appellate Tribunal.[102]

A number of 'higher' or overall structures and instruments for authorising have, however, developed in the Communion as a whole.[103] The Lambeth Conferences have met roughly every ten years since 1867. An Anglican Consultative Council was set up by the Lambeth Conference of

[96]   Lambeth, 1920, p. 77.
[97]   Lambeth, 1930, p. 246.
[98]   S. Van Culin, in *Bonds of Affection*, Proceeds of ACC-6, Anglican Consultative Council (1984), p. 8 and quoted in *Emmaeus*, p. 14.
[99]   Lambeth, 1888, p. 149.
[100] Lambeth, 1908, p. 416.
[101] *Ibid.*, p. 418.
[102] Lambeth, 1978, p. 84.
[103] Lambeth, 1978, pp. 122 ff.

1968, and uniquely among these higher structures has the authority of having its setting up approved by all the provinces of the Anglican Communion. It is not, on the other hand, a body made up of bishops, and its constitutional position was the subject of some disquiet in the debates of the Lambeth Conference of 1988 because it was seen to be in some sense a curial or 'civil service' body, rather than a representative one in any synodical way. The Meeting of Primates was instituted by the Lambeth Conference of 1978.[104] The Archbishop of Canterbury has always had a primatial role in the Anglican structures. (We shall come to the special issue of primacy a little later.) The quartet of 'higher authorities' these represent have only comparatively recently begun to work together, and they are clearly seen as parts of an evolutionary process which is not yet complete.[105] The 1978 Lambeth Conference spoke of the problems which remain in the working out of the relationship of the 'international conferences, councils and meetings within the Anglican Communion'.[106]

The Anglican Consultative Council was designed to carry out the responsibilities which had been entrusted to the Lambeth Consultative Council and the Advisory Council on Missionary Strategy.[107] It was to provide continuity between Lambeth Conferences,[108] and to advise on inter-Anglican relationships at provincial and diocesan level, to develop agreed Anglican policies in the world mission of the Church, to keep before national and regional Churches the importance of the fullest possible Anglican collaboration with other Christian Churches, to encourage and guide Anglican participation in the ecumenical movement.[109] It thus has a double function of providing continuity and advice.[110] These two functions are also found separately in other structures supplementary to the Lambeth Conference or to provincial and diocesan synods. The predominant purpose of a Standing Committee is to ensure continuity in the work of any organ to which it is attached. An *ad hoc* committee or commission is authorised by an officer or body with a continuing commission, to carry out a particular task, and normally to report its findings back to the commissioning body.

---

[104] Lambeth, 1978, pp. 123-4.

[105] Lambeth, 1930, p. 155.

[106] Lambeth, 1978, Resolution 12, p. 42, cf. 1968, p. 145.

[107] Lambeth, 1968, p. 145.

[108] Cf. Lambeth, 1958, I.44 (81).

[109] Lambeth, 1968, pp. 46-7.

[110] Consistent with recommendations of the Conferences of 1920 (Resolution 44) and 1930 (pp. 247-8), about the Consultative Body. The recommendations of the Anglican Consultative Council are like those of Lambeth in that each Provincial Synod takes its own synodical actions in respect of its decisions and recommendations (Lambeth, 1978, p. 102).

The term 'commissioning' is significant here as implying the 'sending' essential to all ministry in the Church. There is in addition a need for a civil service or curia of an administrative sort acting centrally within each province and answering to its provincial or general synod. Such supplementary structures are complementary to meetings which are in their turn supplementary to Lambeth Conferences. The Primates' Meeting is the chief of these.

The notion of the development of the exercise of a wider episcopal fellowship in periodic 'meetings of bishops' of Churches which are in communion with one another, was explored by the Lambeth Conferences of 1948 and 1958, and taken further in 1978, after a congress of 1964 which met 'as an episcopal conference, advisory in character, for brotherly counsel and encouragement', and with the further and larger purpose of constituting a 'comity of bishops in the Church of God, ... who find their sharing in the bishop's office to be a ground of present partnerships and an anticipation of future formal collegial unity in the one universal Church'.[111]

The underlying principle here is that the meeting of bishops is what is constitutive for conciliarity beyond the diocesan level. The 1867 Lambeth Conference underlines 'the right of the Bishops of any Province to meet in Synod by themselves', alongside the recommendation that such a Synod should normally 'consist of the Bishops of the Province, and of representatives both of the Clergy and of the Laity in each Diocese'.[112] The larger idea of a world-wide Anglican Congress has been tried (1954, 1963), but is much too expensive to be practicable very often.[113] The 1968 Conference recommended that such Congresses should be replaced by joint meetings of the Anglican Consultative Council and of Anglican participants in the Assembly of the World Council of Churches, held at the time of that Assembly, and if possible in association with Area Councils of Churches.[114] The formidable difficulties of organising such wide participation has made it plain that the Lambeth Conference (as a meeting of bishops), and the Primates' Meeting, are perhaps the most practical means of securing worldwide consultation, and as means by which the mind of the Anglican Communion may be communicated effectively worldwide.

Although, as the 1978 Conference points out, the Lambeth Conference and the Anglican Consultative Council - and the other supplementary structures and meetings - 'are separate bodies in the life of our Communion', so that 'there is no necessary structural relationship between

111   Lambeth, 1968, pp. 147-8.
112   Lambeth, 1897, p. 60.
113   Lambeth, 1978, p. 104.
114   Lambeth, 1968, p. 145.

the two' on the superficial level,[115] there is a deep structural relationship in the theology of collegiality and conciliarity, and the pattern of diocesan and provincial synodical government out of which they arise. There is also a relationship of shared office or task in the commissioning of the work of the various organs and instruments by the community.

It is on this understanding that we come to the question of primacy. The 1908 Lambeth Conference said that 'no supremacy of the See of Canterbury over Primatial or Metropolitan Sees outside England is either practical or desirable'.[116] The 1930 Conference, in a Committee Report, contrasted as two 'types of ecclesiastical organisation' a 'centralised government' and a 'regional authority within one fellowship'.[117] The 1948 Conference commented that 'former Lambeth Conferences have wisely rejected proposals for a formal primacy of Canterbury'.[118] Yet it has seemed natural in a Lambeth Conference to speak of the See of Canterbury as 'the focal point of our Communion'.[119] This echo of a theology of ministry which makes the ordained minister representative and focus of the life of the community has a further eucharistic echo in a comment of the same Lambeth Conference that 'within the college of bishops it is evident that there must be a president'.[120] It is in accordance with the spirit of the theology of conciliarity and collegiality which we have seen at work within the Anglican Communion that this should be regarded as a 'symbolic primacy' in contrast with a 'primacy of jurisdiction'. That is to say, it is not primarily structural or administrative, but personal and communal, a 'living focus'.[121] That is without prejudice to its having some structural function, as, for example, the Archbishop of Canterbury is seen as a 'permanent link'

---

[115] Lambeth, 1978, p. 102.

[116] Lambeth, 1908, p. 418. In principle, the primacy of the See of Canterbury, which has historical precedent but no constitutional basis, could move elsewhere. The Primate of the Anglican Communion might reside at any appropriate centre of communication. This is important ecumenically, because it underlines the distinction between primacy *per se*, the responsibility held by the minister exercising supreme oversight in the ecclesial body, and a notion of primacy as linked to a particular local church. Some of these issues were raised at the 1988 Lambeth Conference.

On a change of style in Roman Catholic attitudes to primacy and collegiality, see E. Hill, *Ministry and Authority in the Catholic Church* (London, 1988), Chapters 7 and 8.

[117] Lambeth, 1930, Committee Report on the Anglican Communion: 'The Provinces and Patriarchates of the first four centuries were bound together by no administrative bond: the real nexus was a common life resting upon a common faith, common Sacraments, a common allegiance to an Unseen Head. This common life found from time to time an organ of expression in the General Councils.

[118] Lambeth, 1948, p. 84.

[119] Lambeth, 1968, p. 141.

[120] Lambeth, 1968, p. 137.

[121] *Ibid.*, cf. Emmaus, p. 12.

between the Lambeth Conference and the Anglican Consultative Council because he is president of both.[122] To see what is essentially a personal, visible, living authority, a macrocosmic version in the wider Church of the authority of a bishop in the diocese or the priest in the parish, as both representing and focussing and at the same time obedient to the structures through which the community expresses its common mind, is to recognise the respective virtues of each pattern; and what they have to contribute together to a balanced and whole Christian authorising.[123] The understanding of jurisdiction as 'the authority or power necessary for the effective fulfilment of an office' and 'its exercise and limits' as 'determined by what that office involves'[124] dissolves the difficulty some protestants have felt since the sixteenth century about a concept of jurisdiction which appeared in the later Middle Ages to imply personal dominion by prelates. Here again what is personal is also corporate. That is to say, the personal authority which makes the Primate a visible focus, makes him also visibly an expression of the authority of the whole people of God.

The Second Vatican Council set out the principles of a primacy which is conciliar, an expression of *episcope* in the wider Church. Its task is to foster fellowship, by helping all bishops to work together in their task of apostolic leadership both in the local and in the universal Church. The purpose of primacy is to 'help the churches to listen to one another in this way, to grow in love and unity, and to strive together towards the fulness of Christian life and witness; it respects and promotes Christian freedom and spontaneity; it does not seek uniformity where diversity is legitimate, or centralize administration to the detriment of local churches'.[125] This is an ideal towards which the Roman Catholic Church has been moving within the framework of the theology of Vatican II, and which has its visible expression in the Orthodox Churches too, in the style found appropriate by tradition there. The record of the Canterbury Primacy in exercising ministry not in isolation but in collegial association with brother bishops is good. The principle of 'limitation of office' can be seen healthily at work in the Anglican Communion's episcopal and primatial system. There was warm affirmation of that primacy at the 1988 Lambeth Conference. There was also a recognition that 'jurisdiction, being the power necessary for the fulfilment of an office' must vary 'according to the specific functions of each form of *episcope*', so that there may be a 'complementary and

---

122   Lambeth, 1978, p. 102.
123   Cf. Resp. 222.
124   ARCIC A II 16-22, Elucidation 6.
125   ARCIC A I 21.

harmonious working of these different forms of episcope in the one body of Christ'.[126]

---

[126] ARCIC A II 6. Cf. Hammond, *On Schism* (VIII.5, p. 279) on 'subordination', 'of the bishops in every province to their metropolitans; of the metropolitans in every region ... to patriarchs, or primates; allowing also among these such a primacy of order or dignity as might be proportionable'.

Chapter Six

Authority through time

The third plane of the Church's life which intersects with the first two in the person of the bishop, in the tradition of the whole Church up to the sixteenth century, and of those Churches which preserved an episcopal structure thereafter, is that of continuity in time. This ministry has been seen as both symbolising[1] and actually securing in an abiding form, the apostolic[2] character of the Church's mission. Thus one of the things which is meant by the phrase 'historic episcopate' is that historically this ministry has been an organ of the Church's continuity.[3]

There is no question of this continuity of episcopal office being separable from the ecclesial continuity of the community. Luther, who suspected (with some justice) that the episcopate had come to regard itself as an independent and self-perpetuating chain of power in the West, argued for a time that bishops were unnecessary.[4] Other reformers in the sixteenth century and after, did away with episcopacy in the government and ministerial structure of their churches, for much the same reason. Yet it was apparent to the earliest Christians that apostolate cannot exist except in service to the community, and there is no trace in the early period of an authentic ministerial succession being empowered to minister the Word and sacraments independently.

It is in this full ecclesial and communal context that differences are now beginning to be worked out ecumenically. Even in today's divided Church a common baptism has remained a basis of union even where eucharistic communion has for the moment been broken. In this sense we can speak of an unbroken 'apostolic succession' carried in the whole visible Church of the baptised throughout the ages.

We can also be confident that the community of faith remains. Ignatius of Antioch never alludes to a historic succession as the ground of episcopal authority. But he assumes that what orthodox bishops are teaching is what the apostles taught, and that they hold office in a society which is in this way

---

1 Discussed in Niagara.
2 On 'apostolic' see Niagara 54.
3 Cf. 1922 Doctrine Commission, p. 122.
4 On Luther and the Hussites, see pp. 69-70. Cf. Niagara, 19.

continuous with that of Peter and Paul. The second century Church pointed to a publicly verifiable succession of bishops in their churches (and especially to those known to have been founded by the apostles), and to the consensus of all the churches, to demonstrate that authentic Christianity did not embrace the Gnostic and other heretical fantasies of the day. Thus the local churches and their clergy are authentic because they stand in the true and universal succession, which is accordingly a transmission of faith together with that recognised order of ministry which serves it. Irenaeus excludes from the apostolic succession heretics, schismatics, and orthodox bishops of evil life, because they are breakers of faith, of order and of the moral rules.[5]

We have already met the debate over the 'ordinary' and 'extraordinary' character of apostolic office. There is a distinction between that which was 'extraordinary' in the ministry of the first generation, because the apostles were uniquely eye-witnesses; and that which is 'ordinary' and permanent in the ministry of their successors. The refusal of the Church throughout the ages to add to the canon of the Scriptures is a way of underlining this point. In the apostolate certain essential functions could not be handed on; primary apostolic authority is permanently contained in the written records of apostolic literature. But there remains the responsibility for 'maintaining' the Church in the truth and for guardianship of the common faith, and it is this which has been seen as a continuing apostolic task of the community in the ways we have been outlining. This maintenance in the faith is an essential element in the ministry of the Word which we saw the bishop exercising as homilist and teacher in the early Church; we have already touched on the sharing of this ministry in the collegial and conciliar sharing of the episcopal brotherhood; in both there is clearly a special place for a personal *episcope*, that is, for an 'episcopacy' in the strict sense. Our concern here is with its operation over time, that is, with the case for a 'historic episcopate' with special responsibilities in relation to the whole community for the orderly safeguarding of the community's faith and sacramental life which must be handed on from generation to generation.

The difficulty lies not in pointing to the historical evidence for such an episcopate, which is overwhelming throughout most of the centuries of the Church's life and in most parts of the universal Church; but in clarifying what happens in the actual process of 'handing on', especially in relation to the ordaining or consecration of a bishop. This presents problems because of the break in community of sacramental life in the present divided Church. That makes it necessary for the separated communions to find

5   On 'moral rules', see Chapter 9. Niagara, 53 places special emphasis on the community of faith.

ways of recognising the continuing authenticity of one another's ministries when there is thought to have been a failure somewhere in this 'handing on' on one side or both.[6]

Ordination

Here we need to consider not only the handing on of episcopal office, but the whole subject of ordination.[7] All Christian ministry is a gift of the Spirit, a charism. At the same time, it is a service within the community. The Lord and his people own it together. In the case of the ministry with special responsibilities which has come to be known as the 'ordained' ministry, a commissioning of his presbyterial deputies by the head of the community, and an acceptance of the new priests by the people they were to serve, was early coupled with laying on of hands in token of the gift of the Spirit and of continuity. These three elements belong together in ordination. The Pastoral Epistles and Acts 13.3 mention the laying on of hands in the New Testament period, as associated with the giving of the power of the Spirit. 'Do not neglect the spiritual endowment you possess, which was given you, under the guidance of prophecy, through the laying on of the hands of the elders as a body' (I Timothy 4.14, NEB). 'I now remind you to stir into flame the gift of God which is within you through the laying on of hands' (II Timothy 1.6). Ordination is here understood to be a sacramental act conferring a charismatic gift, of grace appropriate to the office. There is no separation here between 'office' and 'gift of the Spirit'. The laying on of hands with prayer in a solemn act is at the same time a recognition of the prophetic call and a sign of the Spirit's gift. Timothy is warned to take good care to act according to the charism bestowed on him (I Timothy 1.18-19; Timothy 6.11-16). Paul reminds the presbyters of Ephesus that their appointment to exercise episcopal oversight comes from the Holy Spirit (Acts 20.28).

The three planes of oversight come together in ordination. The author of the second and third Johannine epistles, 'John the Presbyter', exercised authority not only as a local teacher, but as pastor of a region in which there were a number of churches. Like Timothy and Titus in the Pastoral Epistles, he probably had special responsibilities in ordinations of local clergy; the choice of local congregations would need to be guided if fellowship of the churches with one another was to be maintained. As the authority of the ministry of the local eucharistic community grew more settled; it became natural for the presiding minister in each local church to

---

6   See Niagara, 56, on the arguments about emergency needs.
7   See Niagara 3, 53 and 92.

play a principal role in ordinations of presbyters and deacons in his own church. He would also bear responsibility for them, though always with the people's consent. There was thus a strong and proper local basis for the making of ministers; but at the same time the ancient church understood ordination as more than a local authorisation. The orders of episcopate, presbyterate and diaconate were soon universally extended: for example, a presbyter ordained at Corinth needed only a letter of recommendation by his own bishop to be accepted for ministry in Rome or Ephesus, and allowed to officiate there with the agreement of the local bishop. (The priest, as the bishop's deputy, shares by participation in the laying on of hands in ordination, but he does not - except in circumstances which ancient writers point out as exceptional, himself act as chief officer of the community in ordination.) A newly elected bishop, chosen by his flock, is duly entrusted with the charism of episcopal office by other bishops, who represent universal recognition. This is in line with New Testament record, in which those commissioned to exercise pastoral oversight are appointed by those who themselves have already received the commission.

It is of importance here that although the ordination of a priest is seen as commissioning him for ministry in the universal Church, he is ordained as within a local community by a single bishop. But a bishop's wider responsibility is marked by his ordination by a group of fellow-bishops, and that is inseparably linked to the concept of continuity through time. The Council of Nicaea (325) stipulated that a bishop should be consecrated by the metropolitan with, if possible all the bishops of the province, or at any rate a minimum of three who could represent a wider fellowship. The ordaining bishops ask for the gift of the Spirit for the new bishop's ministry, and by their participation they ensure the historic continuity of his ministry with that of the apostolic Church.[8]

An ordinary and lifelong ministry

Underlying all this is the ancient Church's understanding that the shepherd of the flock is to represent Christ, the Chief Shepherd, whose constancy does not fail. It was an early conviction that God's call in ordination is irrevocable, and the minister commissioned for oversight for life, as a sign of that constancy. An archbishop or Pope may resign or retire, but he does

---

[8] (The three bishops were thought important in this respect by Richard Field, writing *On the Church* in 1606 (p. 155) and by Beveridge.) Beveridge, *Works*, 12, Chapter 2. Cf. Niagara, 91.

not cease to be a bishop.[9] Episcopal office is indelible as the perfecting and highest fulfilment of a priesthood which, although it must in practice be bestowed on the individual before he becomes a bishop, remains in essence a deputed office under that of bishop. This is attested in the sixteenth century Anglican Ordinal (and in more recent forms) by the simple *epiklesis* which commits to the kneeling priest under the hands of the archbishop and other bishops present the responsibilities of the office and work of a bishop in the Church of God. The new bishop's existing priesthood is thus given its wider application and empowered to serve the needs of oversight; and the ordination of bishops may thus be seen as a taking up into brotherhood by the universal episcopate[10] and a dedication to a fuller and perpetual leadership.

In this context must be placed the mediaeval and sixteenth century debate as to whether a bishop is somehow a *sacerdos perfectus* in a way that a priest is not (*perfectus* here meaning 'complete').[11] He is compared in the debates of the Council of Trent with a full-grown man, who is able to beget others like himself, while a priest is likened to a boy who does not possess the power to do so.[12] Scripture seemed to the debaters to be equally balanced here. On the one hand it cannot be said that any superior powers of an episcopal sort were given by Christ at the institution of the Last Supper. On the other hand, Christ's own priesthood 'according to the order of Melchisedek' must be that of a *sacerdos episcopalis*. It can be nothing less, for Christ is Lord. That priests were 'instituted and created to assist the bishops' implied to the Trent fathers that the prime and perfect sacerdotal order is that of bishops.[13] All this is really saying no more than that the office of head of the eucharistic community is the fundamental special or 'ordained' ministry. We find the point made in the sixteenth century when 'governance' and 'ordination' are linked, governance containing a power to ordain.[14] In the seventeenth century the Anglican Hughes suggested that 'the Apostles constituted bishops for the perpetual government of the Church, with a peculiar power of ordination'.[15]

---

[9] It is because of this understanding of its indelibility that episcopal office is already seen as an 'order' in Carolingian times. Congar, *op. cit.*, p. 142, 16th Council of Toledo, 693. See, too, Niagara, 90.

[10] With the proviso in the divided churches that this cannot at present be truly universal.

[11] Cf. Aquinas ST II[ii] q.185, a.1.

[12] Acta CT 9.31.

[13] Acta CT 9.72.

[14] Cf. Acta CT 7[2].467.

[15] Hughes, *Preliminary Dissertation* to Chrysostom, *De Sacerdotio*, Appendix 8 in Hickes, *Christian Priesthood* 3.323-4.

The notion that in bishops was vested a charism given for an office, permanence in that office, and the 'power to ordain' which hands these on from generation to generation, sparked fierce controversy among those sixteenth century reformers who wanted to do away with bishops as usurpers of a power not rightly theirs. Although the Church of England kept firmly to bishops in the sixteenth century, there was a substantial following for the 'presbyterian' view that no episcopal office of any sort was warranted, and in the seventeenth century the need for bishops was widely challenged in England. There is, then, a group of questions to be answered for Anglicans, as well as in an ecumenical context, about the transmission of a historic episcopate through time.

Much of the Reformation disquiet arose from developments in the late antique world and in succeeding centuries which tended to create an imbalance in the understanding of the role the people, that is the community as a whole, played in ordination. If a priest remained a priest, or a bishop a bishop when he served in another community, the local people's role in his ordination could seem insignificant.[16] And during the fourth century the clergy came to play a more prominent role than the laity in the election of a new bishop. In addition, the growth of the notion of grades of ordained ministers in a 'ladder of honour' like a civil service, began to create a sense that there was a barrier between the laity and the president of their diocesan family. The later mediaeval and sixteenth century controversy about the need for episcopal ordination had its roots in these and other changes, which caused ministerial authority to be felt as tyranny by some of the laity; and a reaction ensued which insisted that the people themselves could make ministers without episcopal assistance. It was in this context that, in the sixteenth century, some reformers sought to make a distinction which would have been unintelligible to the early community, between a historic continuity in episcopal office of a linear and unbroken sort, and an apostolicity which consisted solely in adherence to apostolic faith and practice.

Things were brought to a head by the crisis in Bohemia in the fifteenth century over the giving of communion in both kinds to the laity. This had left the Bohemians without a bishop. By Luther's time, the Bohemians could get priests only by sending ordinands to Italy, where they forswore their beliefs, received episcopal ordination, and returned to break their oath and minister wine to the laity. When the Bohemians consulted Luther he

---

[16] Though the rule expressed by Cyprian and enacted at the Council of Nicaea in 325 that each city may have only one bishop remained in force, and the deep sense which the ancient Church had of the intimate bond between a bishop and his own flock persisted. He is still spoken of in the Middle Ages as 'married' to his church. (A number of issues arise in this connection in a uniting Church.)

told them to proceed as the apostles had done in the New Testament, simply
to pray for the guidance of the Holy Spirit, individually and together, and
then to meet to elect those who seemed able and suitable to be ministers.
The leaders of the community are then to lay hands on them and commend
them to the people.[17] The theologians of Trent reacted against such claims
to an exclusively 'popular' making of ministers, which they found in
Calvin's writings as well as Luther's, with the (far from new) assertion that,
on the contrary, the *ius ordinandi,* the power to ordain, lies with bishops
alone.[18] Neither side was denying that the gift of the Spirit is necessary.
They differed only about the manner of its giving.

At issue here was the implication to some reformers' minds that the
imposition of hands by bishops together with an *epiklesis* constituted a claim
to an episcopal power which was independent of the community, and held
by bishops from God as an exclusive, personal possession.[19] In the light of
this anxiety Whitgift comments:

> To use these words, 'Receive the Holy Ghost', in ordering of
> ministers, which Christ himself used in appointing his apostles, is
> no more ridiculous and blasphemous than it is to use the words
> that he used in the supper ... The bishop by speaking these words
> doth not take upon him to give the Holy Ghost, no more than he
> doth to remit sins, when he pronounceth the remission of sins; but
> by speaking these words of Christ, 'Receive the Holy Ghost;
> whose sins so ever ye remit, they are remitted, etc.,' he doth shew
> the principal duty of a minister, and assureth him of the assistance
> of God's Holy Spirit, if he labour in the same accordingly'.[20]

The problem arises only when the balance of personal and corporate in the
actions of the Church is lost sight of, as happened in the West in the later
Middle Ages, and the bishop is no longer clearly seen as serving among and
with his people, but solely as having dominion over them. The laying on of
hands and the invocation of the Holy Spirit in ordination is properly seen as
the action of Christ's representative or representatives in the community.

In the rite of ordination of the 1662 text of the Book of Common Prayer
of the Church of England, candidates are presented to the people and
provision is made for the bishop to ask the people if they know of any
'impediment or notable crime' in the candidate. Each candidate is asked if
he believes himself to be 'truly called' by the Holy Spirit. The archbishop

17 Weimar Ausgabe, 12.193-4.
18 Acta CT 7[2].448 and 9.33. Cf. Melanchthon in CR 8.430 and 12.490.
19 The matter was raised in the Middle Ages (cf. Petrus de Palude, *In Sent.* IV d. 24, q.6 ad
3, printed Venice, 1493, f.130[r]). But it became a focal point of contention in the
sixteenth century and was discussed at the Council of Trent (for example, Acta CT
7[2].440, 468).
20 Whitgift, PS 1.489.

lays hands on the candidate with the declared intention of ordaining him to the episcopate: 'Receive the Holy Ghost for the office and work of a bishop in the Church of God, now committed unto thee by the imposition of our hands', or the bishop lays hands on the candidate with the declared intention of ordaining him to the priesthood. The laying on of hands occurs within a context which is definitive: that is to say, it would be ineffective in isolation; it does not have an automatic or 'magical' character, as some of the reformers feared was being claimed for it in the sixteenth century. The bishop or archbishop acts as within 'the Church of God', that is, the universal Church. Cranmer's paper on the doctrine and discipline of the Church of 1538 is quite clear that Scripture gives a divine institution for such order,[21] and Becon emphasises that it is also necessary for the candidate for ordination to 'submit himself to the judgement of the congregation, either to be admitted or to be refused'.[22] There is a conscious bringing together of human and divine, personal and corporate, authorising here. The priests present join the bishop in the laying on of hands to signify that the commission entrusted to them is shared; the people present signify their assent, and the bishop on behalf of the community prays God to grant the gift of the Holy Spirit to the candidate for a specific purpose. The same pattern, but with bishops sharing in the laying on of hands, occurs in the ordination of a bishop. The prayer and the laying on of hands take place in the context of the Eucharist precisely because ordination is an act in which the whole Church is involved.

Continuity and Succession

We come now to the problems arising from the breakdown of consensus about the theology of ordination, and the consequent damage to a shared continuity of order in some of the protestant Churches at and since the Reformation. Circumstances of division raise a difficulty about universality, in which the problem about 'succession' is embedded. During the Donatist schism in North Africa in the fourth century the general patristic view that there can be no authenticity of ecclesial life outside the catholic Church was already being severely tested. Augustine argues that if valid baptism can be received outside catholic unity, orders may also be unconditionally valid in schismatic communities. But he assumed that the schismatic community would be able to trace its ordinations back to a bishop in linear apostolic succession. Although the bishops who met at Nicaea in 325 would not have thought that a person consecrated by three bishops in

---

[21] *Remains*, PS, p. 484.
[22] Becon, *Catechism*, PS, p. 319.

any circumstances whatever had claims to catholic recognition, it became a habit in the mediaeval West to think of ordination by a bishop in apostolic succession as the exclusive and sole secure test of ministerial and ecclesial validity.[23]

The most serious and lasting division in this respect came about, not with the breach between Eastern and Western Christendom in 1054 but in the sixteenth century. (Orthodox and Roman Catholic communities have been able to continue to accept each other's bishops as authentic.) The circumstances of the Reformation created at least two distinct kinds of difficulty. In the case of the English Church, there was in Anglican eyes no break in fact or intention with the apostolic line, but Roman Catholic commentators argued that such a break had occurred. It was pointed out by Peter Talbot, a Jesuit, in his *A Treatise of the Nature of Catholick Faith and Heresie* (Rouen, 1657), that the sixteenth century Anglican Ordinal merely says 'Take the Holy Ghost'. He argues, in line with the mediaeval concept of the *vis verborum*, the force or effective intention of the words, that because there was no mention of specific office there was nothing in the words 'sufficient to make one a Priest or a Bishop'.[24] The 1662 Ordinal was revised to include the words 'for the office and work of a priest' or 'bishop' to meet this objection.[25] But there continued to be a reservation as to the intention of those who ordained by the old Ordinal. This, taken together with Roman Catholic reservations about the validity of the consecration of Matthew Parker as Archbishop of Canterbury in 1559, at a point crucial for the English 'succession' (and about the theology of priesthood held by sixteenth century Anglicans), culminated in the text of *Apostolicae Curae* in 1896, outlawing Anglican Orders as absolutely null and utterly void.[26] This has created a problem of one-sided recognition. That is to say, Anglicans recognise the validity of Roman Catholic Orders, but the reverse is not at present the case. The second difficulty was of another degree. Some reforming communities in the sixteenth century rejected the need for a personal episcopacy, or even for the need for any sort of oversight or *episcope* at all. In the first case the 'mending' which can bring about mutual recognition of ministry as standing in the apostolic succession depends upon agreement over the validity of certain actions in the past; in the second there is required in addition, an agreement about the nature and role of *episcope* in the community.

23 See L. Saltet, *Les réordinations* (Paris, 1907).
24 p.22.
25 And also objections of a different sort being made by Presbyterian Nonconformists of the day.
26 F.E. Brightman's pamphlet on the Anglican Orders question is still useful.

In the context of the plane of continuity in time we are primarily concerned with the problems raised by a 'linear' notion of an unbroken chain of hands in apostolic succession, in which the person of the bishop has been seen as indispensable for the transmission of the ministerial commission. Certainly, for early Christians, the participation of bishops of other local churches in the consecration of a new bishop was a sign and instrument of the continuity of both the new bishop and his church, with the apostolic communion extended through time and space. This continuity in the ordered life of the community is surely the nerve-centre of the original and continuing concept of apostolic succession. The question is what is in fact indispensable, and whether, once broken, the chain can be mended. Newman was able to see linearity in 'the Royal dynasty of the Apostles' as essentially spiritual. 'Every Bishop of the Church whom we now behold is a lineal descendant of St. Peter and St. Paul after the order of a spiritual birth, a noble thought if we could but realise it,' he comments.[27] The recent Niagara Report of the Anglican-Lutheran International Commission sees the linear succession through persons as only a partial representation of a fuller reality of apostolic succession which takes place in the community as a whole, so that 'episcopal office' may be seen not as consisting 'primarily in an unbroken chain of those ordaining to those ordained, but in a succession which stands in the continuity of apostolic faith and which is overseen by the bishop in order to keep it in the communion of the Catholic and Apostolic Church'.[28]

Such an account of the nature of apostolic succession, which lodges it in the community with its bishop, not in the bishop as such, has the advantage of making it possible to see apostolic continuity in a variety of forms of Church order and ordination. But it depends, for its powers of reconciling differences and mending breaches of communion, upon mutual recognition of the ecclesial reality of separated communions. This is exactly the question Augustine was addressing in his attempt to find a solution to the problem of the Donatist Schism. There the difficulty lay, not in unorthodoxy in the faith on the part of one body, but in a disagreement as to which was the true Church. The Lambeth Conference of 1920, seeking a way of reconciling the episcopal and the non-episcopal Churches, suggested that the visible unity of the Church requires 'a ministry acknowledged by every part of the Church as possessing not only the inward call of the Spirit but also the commission of Christ and the authority of the whole body'. The documents of the Second Vatican Council made a major move forward in this matter of mutual recognition of the ecclesial reality of other

[27] Parochial and Plain Sermons 17, Vol. 3, August 14, 1834.
[28] Niagara 53, quoting LRCJC Ministry in the church, 62.

communions; that is to say, in regarding as 'true Churches' all who share one baptism. In this light it is possible to see the linear succession by laying on of hands as orderly, natural and proper within this full apostolic succession, without 'unchurching' those who have not, or not as yet, found a place for it.[29]

It also suggests a way to the resolution of the difficulty stated by the Lambeth Conference of 1948:

> The most we can say ... for any ministries in the divided Church is that they carry a commission conferred by Christ in and through part of his body but not the whole.[30]

and specifically to the solving of a further kind of difficulty created by the rise of Methodism in the eighteenth century. Because no bishop would ordain his preachers, Wesley - on the grounds that there had been presbyteral ordination in apostolic times - ordained ministers for America in 1784 and for Ireland and Scotland in 1785. This was seen as an emergency measure, but it was one of which his brother Charles disapproved. He wrote to his brother, 'Wesley his hands on Coke hath laid, but who laid hands on him?'[31] There was no intention in Wesley's mind to reject a personal episcopal episcopal ministry, and in world Methodism bishops have been appointed in certain areas. The problem of reconciliation of ministry here lies, not in finding a way to bring together differently conceived ministerial orders, but in dealing with the consequences of emergency action, taken independently of the community as a whole. It thus has some similarities in its consequences with the situation created by the appointment of women as bishops when the Church as a whole is not able to accept them.

On a view of the apostolic succession as maintained in the whole community there is nothing to 'mend', no 'broken line', but there remains a question which continues to separate 'episcopal' and 'non-episcopal' churches about the character of episcopal office. In the sixteenth century Richard Hooker could regard the institution of bishops as 'from heaven, even of God, and say that the Holy Ghost was the author of it'.[32] He saw it

---

[29] See for example, Hickes, *Two Treatises*.

[30] The Committee Report on the Unity of the Church, Appendix on 'Supplemental Ordination'. William Goode thought it 'The great question', 'whether it is a doctrine of the Church of England that Episcopal Ordination is a *sine qua non* to constitute a valid Christian ministry' ('Non-episcopal Ordination'. from an article in the *Christian Observer*, Nov., 1851, republished London, 1856).

[31] Quoted in Horton Davies, *Worship and Theology in England, 1690-1850* (Princeton, 1961), p. 207.

[32] Laws VII.v.10.

as the form of church government which best agrees with Scripture.[33] Whitgift says much the same in his controversy with Cartwright. Episcopacy, he says, is 'an order placed by the Holy Spirit in the Church'.[34] The Puritans hated such language. For William Ames, whose Calvinism was so rigorous that he had to live in the Netherlands, the episcopal order seemed merely one among a number of possible ways of forming a ministerial structure, all equally valid. Some puritans could belong in conscience to the Church of England provided bishops were thought of in this way, as a mere convenience.

The 'historic episcopate'

One line of argument designed to help here, and successively explored by Lambeth Conferences in connection with the Chicago-Lambeth Quadrilateral of 1886-8, has been to rest the case on history. The Quadrilateral speaks in the last of its four clauses of 'the historic episcopate'.[35] Dr. Vincent, Assistant-Bishop of Southern Ohio, was anxious in the debates of the 1880s to make it plain that the phrase 'the historic episcopate' was chosen because it described a 'fact'.[36] The Report of the Joint Commission on Approaches to Unity in the American General Convention of 1949 saw episcopacy 'not as a bare fact, but a fact accompanied by its historical meaning'. It is, in other words, a fact invested with significance by the context of life and worship in which it has been a reality in the greater part of the Christian Church for two thousand years. It is, one might say therefore, a fact carrying doctrinal implications. The 1920 Lambeth Conference in its Resolution 9 (vi and vii) asks, 'May we not reasonably claim that the Episcopate … is the one means of providing … a ministry acknowledged by every part of the Church as possessing not only the inward call of the Spirit, but also the commission of Christ and the authority of the whole body?' and 'the best instrument for maintaining the unity and continuity of the Church?' The case here rests on the presence of a personal episcopate throughout most of the Church for most of its history, as having ensured and guaranteed universal faithfulness to the apostolic truth. Newman speaks eloquently of the meaning of this historical reality. 'The presence of every Bishop,' he says, 'suggests a long history of conflicts and trials, sufferings and victories, hopes and fears, through many centuries … he is the 'living' monument of those who are dead … we see their figures

33 *Ibid.* III.xi.16. Cf. Niagara, 20.
34 Whitgift PS II.405.
35 See my article in *Quadrilateral at One Hundred*, ed. J. Robert Wright, *Anglican Theological Review* (1988); cf. Niagara, 3.
36 Cf. ARCIC A I (3) and Encyclical Letter of Lambeth 1888.

on our walls, and their tombs are under our feet; and we trust, nay we are sure, that God will be to us in our day as he was to them'.[37]

But it is important not to let the poetry of what Newman says cloud the fundamental question of the satisfactoriness of the argument from the facts of history. The Quadrilateral states facts, and in relation to the episcopal order lays stress on the historicity of the fact. This fact is also asserted to be a norm for life and unity because, for the Anglicans who first drafted the four articles, it seemed clear that the episcopal order is important, since to keep it as sign of sacramental authenticity in due succession is also to make a statement about the continuity of the Church in history. The Lambeth Bishops of 1888 left the Quadrilateral open to criticism from non-episcopal Churches, that they themselves were by implication unchurched because they did not share the same sense of the continuity of Christian history and of the episcopate as its sign.

To say that the episcopate is not essential, but is nevertheless a God-given norm and a practical vehicle of the continuity of the Church's ordained ministry, takes us some way towards a resolution of the objection that something can be said to be 'missing' in the ministries of the non-episcopal Churches, or in Churches where there has been at some point a break with the old succession and the institution of a fresh 'episcopate'.[38] Mutual ecclesial recognition is a prerequisite, and that presupposes mutual recognition that we share a common faith. Then we may begin to look towards the finding of means by which all our ministries may act, as the Appeal of the Lambeth Conference of 1920 puts it, 'throughout the whole fellowship'. This approach identifies what is 'lacking' as a rejection of communion with an apostolic and catholic tradition which must remain one in the universal Church. Thus the 'defect' is one of universality; not a technical fault of pedigree but an isolation from the organic spiritual life in shared faith, of the one holy, catholic and apostolic Church. Such a view accords with a picture of apostolic succession as carried by the whole community. It helps us to get away from a tendency to take in isolation various possible 'defects' and to seek to define technical faults as making others' ministries 'invalid'.

We have been concentrating upon the acute and knotty problem raised by a conception of ordination as a means by which authority in the Church is carried on over time, on the understanding that it is in the person who is the community's ordaining officer that the three planes of the Church's life intersect, and who is the instrument bringing together charism and office in

[37] Parochial and Plain Sermons 17, Vol. 3, Aug. 14, 1834.
[38] As in some Lutheran Churches. The Appeal of the Lambeth Conference of 1920 is one of a number of examples of proposals for making good a presumed 'defect'.

the commissioning of the ordained ministry for service in the community. When certain groups of sixteenth century reformers tried to disjoin the two, they were arguing only that the imposition of hands could effect no automatic transmission of sacramental grace through the line of apostolic ministry. It seemed to them that the Holy Spirit could be given, at the prayer of the community, with its leaders. But the result was in fact a radical disjoining of charism and office. That may be said without prejudice to the fact that the ministries thus commissioned had, and have, an unquestionable spiritual reality; for the Holy Spirit can and does act directly in commissioning for ministry, and such an independent pastorate may be blessed by God as an efficacious means of proclaiming the Gospel. But it separates ordination from universal order. That is of course only one of many threads in the fabric of order in the Church. There has been a pervasive awareness of the need to keep faith with the past in the decrees of councils. Councils have normally renewed and reaffirmed what their predecessors have done. Lanfranc, Archbishop of Canterbury, called the Council of London which met in 1075, and presided there; and 'many things were renewed, which are known to have been defined by old canons, because councils had been disused in the kingdom of England for many years past' (Johnson, II.12-13). There has been an anxiety, as strong among reformers of the sixteenth century as anywhere else, to show that they are not 'innovators' but true to the apostolic pattern in their faith and worship. In liturgy and life, faith and order alike, every ecclesial community has always and everywhere sought to maintain what is apostolic. That is the essence of the continuity of Christian authority over time (cf. Lambeth, 1978, p. 98).

The study of the New Testament will not provide, as perhaps sixteenth and seventeenth century Anglican divines believed, a warrant for the view that a three-fold ministry of a wholly fixed type is a proper and necessary ecclesial foundation. But it does clearly show how naturally that ministry gradually came into being, how useful and practical it proved, and how it met the needs of the communities for means of ensuring continuity over time, when that became important after the first generation. There was then, and remains, room for variety of form in this three-fold ministry. '*Episcope* or oversight concerning the purity of apostolic doctrine, the ordination of ministers and pastoral care of the Church is inherent in the apostolic character of the Church's life, mission and ministry. This has been embodied and exercised in the Church in a wide variety of forms'.[39] The same has been true of the diaconate as a ministry of practical and administrative service and of service at the eucharistic table; and of the local

---

[39] A-L, Pullach, 79, in *Growth*.

pastoral office held under the ministry of the whole people of God. The threefold ordained ministry forms a complex, flexible and durable structure of authority in matters of order in most communions, and it has never been seriously challenged among Anglicans except in the period of the debate with the presbyterians which was at its height in the seventeenth century. In the modern Anglican Communion, the bishop-in-synod, with clergy and laity, has become a paradigm of the order which makes the ministry of the whole people of God a single offering.

Chapter Seven

The Ordination of Women: a Note on the Ecclesiology

In ordination three things come together: the gift of the Holy Spirit; the community's acceptance of the new minister's standing in a special relationship to the community; the bringing of the candidate into a recognised place in the Church's order, with certain offices, tasks and responsibilities. There are at present uncertainties in relation to each of these in the debate over the ordination of women. We cannot know as yet whether the gift of the Holy Spirit for the office and work of a priest or bishop in the Church of God is given to women, although in Churches where they have been ordained experience strongly suggests that it is. Secondly, we can see that while some local communities welcome women priests and bishops, some do not, or do not yet do so. There is no unanimity about this either way, and decisions either for or against always at present override the wishes of some. There is the further difficulty that the 'title' or actual pastoral charge which ought always to be associated with the conferring of orders is in practice limited at present in the case of a woman by local willingness to accept her as pastor. So the position about the community's acceptance is unclear, and even confused. Thirdly, it is clear that women cannot at present enter fully into the Church's order, and that their ordination must destroy that order because, as things stand, it is impossible for them to have a place in that order which everyone recognises.

If this is a right description, there must be some doubt as to whether it is at present ecclesiologically possible for women to be ordained as priests or bishops 'in the Church of God'.[1] It should be stressed that these ecclesiological questions arise only because we do not know whether women can be ordained in the sight of God; they therefore rest upon different criteria from those customarily used in the discussion of possible theological objections to the ordination of women which seem for the moment to have

---

[1] Except in a Church which has a congregational rather than an episcopal structure, for the third element in ordination is looked at rather differently where 'the Church in each place' is regarded as the Church's only visible manifestation.

brought us to an impasse. They are, however, every bit as difficult to
resolve.

The Anglican Church has been regarded as a bridge-Church between the
protestant and Roman Catholic and Orthodox traditions. With the
ordination of its first woman bishops it becomes for the first time a Church
seeking to embrace in one Communion the two hitherto irreconcileable
traditions of order: that which places the emphasis on the congregation as
calling and appointing ministers under the Holy Spirit; and that which sees
ordained ministry as ministry in the universal Church and requires
episcopal ordination (on the understanding that that implies universal
acceptance in any congregation, on the recommendation of the ordaining
bishop and with the consent of the bishop of the diocese where the ordained
minister is to serve, as well as of the local congregation). This is the
unavoidable consequence of any legislative provision which seeks to
safeguard local wishes at the expense of universal order: whether in
independent action by a province; or in provisions made for the pastoral
needs of congregations within a province. The positive side to this change is
that it greatly sharpens the need to work with non-episcopal Churches on the
place of episcopal ministry in a future united Church; the negative side is
that it sets the Anglican Church substantially further apart from Orthodox
and Roman Catholic understandings of ministerial order. But above all, it
makes the Anglican Church not a single Communion seeking unity with
others, but itself an ecumenical crisis zone, in which the desire for unity
struggles to hold together what structural anomalies pull apart. That must
be frankly confessed.

The present problem within the Anglican Communion points up a perhaps
unprecedented difficulty. If it can be argued that the *esse* of the Church
lies in its unity, its holding together (and that is as true for the 'gathered
believers' of a Congregationalist system as for Churches with a wider 'local'
basis such as Lutheran Landeskirchen and Anglican dioceses and provinces),
then internal division at the point where that holding together is structurally
articulated must threaten the *esse* of the Church. I have argued that the
bishop in an episcopal Church has traditionally been the minister in whose
person unity is maintained on three planes. The first is the presidency of
the eucharistic community. The bishop is still in principle the head of the
eucharistic community of his diocese. (That is why he confirms those
baptised by his priests.) But if there is to be be variation from parish to
parish in the acceptance of women priests, and if a woman bishop cannot act
as head of the diocesan eucharistic community for some of her people
because they are unable to accept the validity of her ministry, this primary
pastoral role is damaged. The second is the plane which unites the Church
in each place with the universal Church. Here again, where there is not
universal recognition of a woman bishop by other bishops, there is a breach

of unity. The third plane is that of continuity through time. Here, there are clearly going to be difficulties about the acceptance of women bishops as able to maintain that continuity in their own persons and participate in handing it on. The three planes cannot intersect in the person of every bishop in our Communion as they have done in the past.

There would seem to be some implications for the understanding of the indelibility of ordination. That is important, for it is only if ordination is understood to confer an indelible character that we are in perpetual difficulties about the status of ordinations about whose validity not everyone can agree. Anglicans would certainly not want to query the indelibility of an ordination in which all can see all three elements present. But it may be argued that where that has not been the case a subsequent liturgical act can be seen, not as throwing doubt on the gift of the Spirit or repairing a defect, but as making visible to the whole community the fullness of an ordination in which the Holy Spirit, the people of God locally and the people of God universally all play their parts. Entered into in a spirit of humility, as waiting upon God, such a service of reconciliation of ministries may mend our unity when in due time it becomes clear beyond question what is the will of God for the ministry of women.

In the meantime, there is the problem of recognition. To take the question of local authority first. No individual can either 'recognise' or not recognise as validly ordained, a minister ordained within the agreed order of the Church, because ordained ministry - like all Christian ministry - is of and within the community and has reference only to the community. The local congregation, in Anglican practice, has a say in the choosing and making of ministers, which is marked in the service of ordination by the participation of the people at certain points.[2] There is some variation provincially here,[3] especially in the election of bishops. Between the point at which a particular candidate is settled on, and the receiving of the new bishop in the cathedral church of the diocese by the people, comes a service of ordination or consecration, which has more than a local reference. That is the reason for the ancient tradition that at least three bishops must join in the making of a new bishop, in token that this is an office in the universal Church. It follows that when the local people welcome their new pastor they too are acting as members of the believing community, and on behalf of the whole people of God. There is an obvious difficulty about the consecration of a bishop who for some reason cannot be deemed to be thus

[2]   See both The Book of Common Prayer and the Alternative Service Book for the Church of England. The principle is sustained in the ordinals of all Anglican provinces.

[3]   In the Episcopal Church of the United States of American, for example, the procedure is electoral. See *Church and State*, Chapter III on the procedure in the Church of England. There was similar variation in the Middle Ages in different parts of Europe.

consecrated to an office 'in the Church of God'.[4] If what is argued in this study about the 'higher rule' of collegiality and conciliarity is right, the merely local act is *ipso facto* imperfect. The question of continuity in time[5] is not immediately affected, but it will inevitably be affected in the future until universal recognition may become possible.[6]

Those provinces of the Anglican Communion in which there are already women priests and where the normal procedures of appointment can now result in local election of a woman as bishop, are placed thereby in a position which has a series of consequences. These follow not as a result of censure on the part of other provinces,[7] but as unavoidable results. The diocese is to a greater or lesser degree isolated, because a group of priests and deacons comes into being, ordained by a bishop whose power to ordain is not accepted everywhere in the Communion. (This is a much more obstinate problem to resolve than that posed by a situation where women ordained in one province are not allowed to serve as ordained ministers in another.) The people of the community as a whole are affected by the decision as communion is impaired.[8] Some individuals feel in conscience that they must worship elsewhere, in another diocese, or that they must regretfully cease to be Anglicans, because they are not clear that the change in the subject of ordination does not take Anglican out of the catholic tradition. The whole Anglican Communion is placed in difficulties arising from the fact that the three planes can no longer intersect in the person of certain bishops, because of the broken continuity of the local and universal dimension. Collegiality and conciliarity are damaged. The universal Church is for the time being further fragmented and placed some steps back on the road to unity by an addition to the problems of mutual recognition of ministries which already exist.

What has been said here has reference only to the aspects of order with which this study is chiefly concerned. There are many for whom there appears to be an over-riding imperative to redress an imbalance by ending the exclusion of women from the priesthood and the episcopate. They would argue that until that is done, ministry in the Church is incomplete and

---

4 See Book of Common Prayer formula.
5 See Chapter 6.
6 It should be noted that at the Lambeth Conference of 1988 it was clear that in many parts of the Communion the ordination of women is not yet a pressing question, or even on the agenda. It is of some importance not to allow a false sense of urgency to rush us. This in itself is an element in the Church's responsibilities over time, that is, to allow development to go at the pace appropriate to the needs of the faithful.
7 As the Lambeth 1988 Resolution I stresses.
8 'Impaired Communion' is not the same as the breaking of Communion because the Churches involved do not identify themselves as separated ecclesial bodies. On the other hand, the concept of 'degrees of communion' is unsatisfactory.

does not reflect the fullness of Christ's humanity. That, too, is an ecclesiological argument and it would not be right to end this note without mentioning it.

Chapter Eight

Authority in matters of faith

The issue of 'defining' matters of doctrine loomed large in the discussion which preceded the calling of the second Lambeth Conference of 1877. The anxiety about 'interference' with the proper sphere of jurisdiction of independent provinces had not been entirely allayed by the provisions discussed in 1867, or by the Resolution about the subordination of diocesan to provincial synods. 'We have no desire to interfere with their affairs, and I am sure they have no desire to interfere in ours,' the Archbishop of Canterbury reassured Convocation in April, 1875.[1] 'The present state of the Christian Church makes men more than usually sensitive as to any appearance even of a claim on the part of any one branch of the Church to interfere with the decisions or administrations of another,' he wrote to the American bishops in June, 1875.[2] It was feared that the agenda might be taken over and changed by a determined party of bishops, and the Archbishop wrote letters asking for suitable topics to be submitted in advance, so that this might be prevented. The theme of his letters was the narrow band of concerns which were adjudged to lie in the proper sphere for discussion at a Lambeth Conference if matters of discipline were ruled out as belonging to independent provincial legislation,[3] and matters of doctrine were also not allowable; for if the Conference was not to be a Council, it could not be thought to perform a conciliar function in articulating a common mind on matters of faith.

But the arguments of the Archbishop had a rather different thrust. His point was that Anglicans already have a common faith. 'Our doctrines are contained in our formularies.'[4] In a letter to the Bishop of Pittsburgh (April 27th, 1875) he says that 'there was a general feeling that matters of doctrine which are already settled by our formularies could not be reopened.'[5] To the American bishops he wrote in June, 'It appears to us that, respecting matters of doctrine, no change can be proposed or discussed

---

1   Davidson, Origin and History of the Lambeth Conferences, p. 19.
2   Ibid., p. 109.
3   On the question of discipline, see Authority in Moral Matters.
4   Ibid., p. 18.
5   Ibid., p. 107.

and that no authoritative explanation of doctrine ought to be taken in hand.'[6] There is already a distinct sense that provincial autonomy is at stake here too. 'Our formularies are interpreted by the proper judicial authorities,' he said to Convocation.[7] 'Each Church is naturally guided in the interpretation of its formularies by its recognised authorities,'[8] he wrote to the American bishops. Both these assumptions beg questions, and these questions are the subject of this chapter.

The Committee appointed by the ensuing Lambeth Conference of 1878 to look into the best mode of maintaining union underlined the importance of Anglican unity in 'one faith' and 'through the ministry of the same Apostolic Orders', but at the same time it spoke of the 'right' of each province, acting (it is implied) as a Church, to change ceremonies and rites 'ordained only by man's authority'.[9] This has reference to Articles 20 and 24 of the Thirty-Nine Articles, which speak of 'rites and ceremonies' and 'traditions' in the light of sixteenth century controversy on this point, and of related concerns to which we shall come in due course.[10] What is not clear either from the Thirty-Nine Articles or from the 1878 Conference Report is whether the 'ministry of the same Apostolic Orders' falls under the heading of 'one faith' or whether any part of the rules governing Orders may be considered a question of 'rite', 'ceremony' or 'tradition' of a sort proper for independent legislation by a province.[11] To conform with the spirit of the Articles any independent action of that kind ought to defer to 'common authority' (*publica auctoritas*) locally, and be framed so as to avoid troubling consciences.

It is plain that the Lambeth Conferences' dilemma over decision-making in matters of faith touched far deeper issues than those which created the immediate difficulties. The first question was whether there was a job of decision-making to do at all, and if so, exactly what it was. That is to say, whether, as one Anglican writer of the later nineteenth century put it, whether the authority of the Church in matters of faith is 'declarative', 'definitive', 'prescriptive' or even perhaps 'originative'.[12] The 1968

---

[6] Ibid., p. 109.

[7] Ibid., p. 18.

[8] Ibid., p. 109.

[9] Ibid., pp. 118-19.

[10] William Beveridge, *Ecclesia Anglicana*, p. 118, picks out the 'decreeing of ceremonies' and 'the determining of controversies' as the two things which belong to the Church's authority. See, too, Proceedings of the General Synod of the Church of England, 15 Nov., 1984, p. 1135, 'There is such a thing as development in doctrine and there can also be development in order and in the understanding of order'.

[11] Cardwell, *Synodalia* I.14 and 30, 49.

[12] Ball, p. 21.

Lambeth Conference spoke of 'showing forth' and 'proclaiming';[13] more recent Anglican authors have thought the Church's task not one of 'continuous revelation, but a continuous interpretation',[14] and given it a 'limited but creative role'.[15]

Something has already been said about this ancient and persistently troublesome issue of the role of the Church in establishing authority in matters of faith in our first chapter, in connection with the authority of Scripture. We must now look at the additional implications of what we have been saying about order. The first principle to emerge is that there must be here the same complementarity of ascending and descending authorising as in the broad field of the Church's ordering of her common life of which this is a part. We should also expect to find the same healthy tension of what is sometimes called central and dispersed authorising. The 1867 Lambeth Conference was anxious to recognise the first in its exploration of the role of clerical and lay consultants and advisers.[16] The second is set out at length in the 1948 Conference's description of authority in matters of faith as 'single in that it is derived from a single Divine source' but also 'distributed' among Scripture, Tradition, Creeds, the Ministry of the Word and Sacraments, the witness of saints, and the *consensus fidelium*, which is the continuing experience of the Holy Spirit through his faithful people in the Church, 'dispersed' in having 'many elements which combine, interact with, and check each other'.[17] Scripture, with tradition, reason and experience, fits into this framework of two axes of authority in the Church. Scripture with the early tradition of the Church are sources, a 'given', and in a sense a 'descending' authority in matters of faith. But Scripture is a living and present authority in the Church's worship and preaching and study and reflection, and continuity in tradition make that, too, a living and present authority. Reason and experience might be said to belong to an 'ascending' authorising. They are means by which the Holy Spirit brings individuals to a recognition of truth, and they operate even in the multitude of the faithful down the centuries who have had no direct access to Scripture in their own tongue, but whom we cannot regard as thus disenfranchised as Christian decision-makers.

The present-day style of Anglican decision-making is 'consultative',[18] a deliberate keeping in balance of 'ascending' and 'descending' elements in

---

13 Lambeth, 1968, pp. 82-3.
14 McAdoo, in *Christian Authority*, p. 253.
15 *The Nature of Christian Belief*, p. 7, speaking of the Creeds.
16 Lambeth, 1867, p. 2.
17 Lambeth, 1948, pp. 84-5.
18 The Constitution of the Anglican Consultative Council gives it brief in terms of 'sharing information, 'advising', 'developing as far as possible agreed policies', 'encouraging',

which stress is laid upon mutual courtesy and the recognition of equality. This combination of order and freedom is of course not unique to Anglicanism. It includes a number of features very ancient in Christian decision-making: the recognition of the community's 'right and sometimes duty ... to engage in critical discussion of decisions on faith and morals';[19] a concern always essential to the catechumenate, to encourage every Christian as far as his or her capacity allows to learn about the faith; respect for Christian scholarship; all that is contained in the early Church's picture of Christ the Teacher who encourages and stretches his pupils and listens to and respects what right response they are able to make. The use of modern media of communication makes it possible for issues to be discussed very widely.[20] There is today a quite proper call by lay people for means of participating actively in the consultative process not merely as respondents to proposals put before them in deanery and diocesan and higher synods, but in the framing of proposals and in the formulation of statements of doctrine. (The 1978 Lambeth Conference encouraged the setting up of an inter-Anglican Theological and Doctrinal Advisory Commission for an experimental five years.)[21] These are parts of a machinery for articulating the common mind which is not yet working as efficiently as it might, but which recognise that 'authority, if it is to be effective, must gain consent, and consent can only be gained where those involved have been able to take part'.[22] It is reception and 'consent' and the question of its 'effect' and 'powers' in Christian decision-making which we must look at first.

The mutual correction and corporate maintaining of the larger community in the faith and in order by those exercising episcope, acting not only on behalf of, but also *with* their communities, can be seen as early as Acts 15. It was already apparent there that meetings of leaders do not stand on their own either as making decisions independently, or as involving only the leaders. At the first Council in Jerusalem, Paul and Barnabas came from Antioch and met the leaders of the Jerusalem community for discussion. Their conclusions were evidently accepted by the Jerusalem community as a whole, for the message which was sent back with Paul and Barnabas came from the apostles and elders together with the whole Church (Acts 15.22). The letter was read in Antioch to the whole community (Acts 15.30). That does not imply that a merely passive role is proper for the

---

'guiding', 'keeping in review' (Lambeth, 1968, p. 466 ff.). The result has been 'an emphasis on process rather than the juridical' (McAdoo).

19 Resp. 249.

20 Cf. Lambeth, 1958 and 1968 and even 1978 (p. 85) on the problems this can raise.

21 Lambeth, 1978, Resolution 25, p. 47. This is a development of the mediaeval function of university teachers.

22 Suenens, *Dossier*, p. 16.

laity. The special episcopal responsibilities are without prejudice to the duty of every Christian to participate in the ministry of the Word; the practicalities of learning and teaching and making decisions within the community are all to be seen as parts of the ministry of a Word which is a living and present authority in the Church's worship and preaching and study and reflection. The declaration of faith in baptism from its earliest forms requires the candidate to make an intellectual assent as well as a commitment, and to express his or her faith to himself and the community as well as to God. There has always been room for teachers who are not among those entrusted with oversight in the community, from the early 'prophetic ministers' to the academic or professional theologian. At the Council of Trent in the sixteenth century deputations were sent from the universities of Europe, and theologians debated freely alongside bishops. Today's equivalent is the Commission or Committee, on which bishops, clergy, lay people and scholars (who may be bishops, clergy or lay people), are brought together to give balanced consideration to a problem and to pool their expertise. There is room for every kind of teaching skill which is a gift of the Spirit and the crêche held for the smallest children during worship in a church is of equal importance before God with an international commission. But an individual may speak focally and representatively for the Church only within the formal structure of its ministry, either as an ordained minister, or at the invitation of someone who has pastoral care of souls.

The role of the laity

The active participation of the laity has not always been possible in practice. In the late antique world higher education was not restricted to the Christian clergy. Augustine contended with articulate and sophisticated philosophers among the pagans who wanted to know why a Christian Roman Empire had been allowed by its God to fall to pagan invaders. But after the time of Gregory the Great at the beginning of the seventh century a clerical monopoly grew up, as Christian scholars became the preservers and carriers of ancient and early Christian learning in a violent age (Benedict Biscop and Bede in particular in England). Charlemagne encouraged the giving of serious attention to the education of the cathedral clergy, and in monastic schools all over Europe the reading of Scripture and the Fathers was kept alive, with some vestiges of classical studies. By the late eleventh century things were sufficiently settled for an articulate middle class laity to make itself heard. Throughout the later mediaeval centuries their voices are raised in protest at what had by now become a virtual exclusion of the laity from direct access to Scripture in a language they could understand. Much was changed by sixteenth century developments, especially in northern

Europe; but the reformers found that lay reading of the Bible, and the exercise of private judgement, was not without its drawbacks from the point of view of maintaining orthodoxy, and that a problem was arising over the control of proliferating and various reforming opinions. It is this heritage of resentment at exclusion of the laity, followed by an encouragement to more or less freedom of personal opinion in reaction with which we are still struggling in trying to arrive at the right balance. It is much more difficult in practice to proceed on a basis of universal free agreement than on a basis of giving clear instructions from above. There was also the ecclesiological difficulty that neither reformers nor conservatives in the sixteenth century were able to see the Church as a fellowship in which the active, conscious, informed and responsible collective judgement of the whole body of the faithful is not only an inseparable part (that was understood) but a necessary *practical* part of the process of 'authorising'.

We can see the beginning of an attempt to work out the mechanics of this process in a comment of Newland. 'Every individual has a right to search the Scriptures, and form his own opinion as to their doctrines', he says, 'and if he exercises that right in humility and sincerity, he is justified in expecting the guidance of heaven ... now the same rights attend a body of men. If their deliberations are conducted with diligence and in prayer, it is reasonable to suppose that they will come to just conclusions'.[23] The idea is to be found already in 1547 in the Address of the Canterbury Synod: 'The clergy desireth that such matters as concerneth religion, which be disputable, may be quietly and in good order reasoned and disputed ... in this house, whereby the verities of such matters shall the better appear. And the doubts being opened and reasonably discussed, men may be fully persuaded with the quietness of their consciences.'[24] There is something more here than the conception we have already met, that a properly constituted council or synod will be guided by the Holy Spirit; there is the expectation that every Christian mind individually will be 'fully persuaded', so that there may be unanimity and the winning of minds, and so that those who take part in the decision-making can witness together. There is still a long way to go to make this a working reality, but it seems plain that in this fullest *consensus fidelium* alone can there be a perfecting *quoad nos* of that which is complete and perfect in its truth but still in process of being appropriated by the Christian community age by age.

It might be convincingly argued that what is needed is not a thoroughgoing systematisation of the role of the whole people of God but rather a clear recognition of its indispensability, and the development of as

[23] Newland, p. 311.
[24] Cardwell, *Synodalia*, II.423.

many and various ways of exercising it as possible. In other words, a balance of the formal and the informal is as important as a balance of the roles of oversight and of consensus, ordained and lay ministry, expert and general knowledge. Councils and synods exist for formal consultative decision-making. And just as ordination to a ministerial office is the entrusting of authority to be used for a specific and limited purpose within the *koinonia*, so the convening of meeting, which involves a 'collective office' is the entrusting of a limited authority for a limited purpose within the *koinonia*. This limiting intention, perhaps rather than its 'representativeness', defines the scope of the authority of the meeting; for within the *collegium* of the whole community, all orderly meetings involve representation.[25]

Reception

What is brought about by a meeting of any sort is therefore in a formal sense limited by its brief.[26] Its informal effects or influence are another matter, as gradual and diverse as the response of the faithful must always be within the full *collegium* of the community. We see this twofold character in the authority of the 'Ecumenical' or 'General' Councils. They have made decisions on questions of discipline and of fundamentals of doctrine and on controverted matters which have been widely and seriously debated, with the intention of providing a definitive ruling to which the whole Church may look. The whole Church has gradually made its response, in confirmation by principal sees, and also by the acceptance and active embracing of such definitions by the faithful as a whole. Such a Council has sought to express what it understood to be the mind of the Holy Spirit in the mind of the Church (cf. Acts 15.28), and its authority has become clear not only from the circumstances of its convening and meeting, but also *ex post facto* from its reception. 'The real test of the ecumenicity of a Council,' says Tyrrell Green in the nineteenth century, consists in the reception of such Council and its work by every portion of the Church. The Divine Spirit is promised to the whole Church, and the consentient witness of the whole Church is therefore necessary'. He thus brings into the foreground not the question of legitimate convening and the proper conduct of a meeting, but the question of reception, and sets the role of the Holy Spirit in its larger context in the response of the whole Church to the decrees of a Council. He does so without ignoring the importance of order in the calling

---

25 ARCIC A II (16-21) and Resp. 248, cf. *Codex Iuris Canonici* 145 (i). Officium ecclesiasticum est quolibet munus ... consituta in finem spiritualem exercendum.

26 The principle applies equally to the way a committee is appointed to carry out a task and offer its finds back to the commissioning body.

and holding of Councils. 'Synods,' he says, 'are the regular machinery for registering agreement of the Church', but their authority 'only becomes decisive after their verdict has been accepted by the Church at large'. He also puts the whole process into place in relation to Scripture. 'A general Council is summoned to declare what has always been the faith, not to propound a new faith. The faith has been once and for all delivered (Jude 3), and enshrined in Holy Scripture, which is thus the Church's standard of doctrine; nothing may, therefore, be taught as an article of faith unless it be traceable to the Holy Scripture'.[27] T.I. Ball makes the same key point about reception. The test of ecumenicity is 'the reception accorded to the decisions of the Council by the whole Church'. 'This comes from the fact that the real power of the Church is resident in the whole body.'[28]

The binding force of their decisions does not, then, lie in the legislative powers of Councils, at which we shall be looking in the chapter on moral authority. The effect of legislative decisions, whether taken by ecumenical or General Councils, or provincial synods, works by 'receiving' in the life of the Church.[29] This reception is not simply response and affirmation, but entails an embodying of what is affirmed in the lived experience of the community. It is this reception in its fullest sense which is the ultimate indication that the Church's authoritative decision in a matter of faith has been truly preserved from error by the Holy Spirit.[30] That requires perfect consensus, a unanimity we can as yet only glimpse, and which goes much further than 'getting the feeling of a meeting' or even the gracious giving way of one dissenter in a consensus in the Society of Friends.[31]

Aristotle saw consent as a principle of verification. For Euclid and Boethius alike, the *communis animi conceptio* is a truth attested by universal acceptance[32] as being apparent to all reasonable minds. Among the earliest Anglican authors the theology of consent and reception is relatively undeveloped.[33] We find Calfhill in 1565 touching on the principle of

27 Tyrrell Green, p. 140.
28 Ball, pp. 124-5.
29 Cf. *Codex Iuris Canonici*, which says that a particular Council can make law and has power of governance, with due regard for the universal law of the Church (445). Cf. Henry Hammond, Of Heresy, p. 339. 'If the sentence of a major part of bishops in a council be not, when it comes to be declared to the world, admitted or received in the Church, as consonant to the doctrine of the Apostles ... this evidently prejudiceth the authority of that council, and shows their incompetence for the work in hand of universal testification.'
30 Resp. 224.
31 See Wilberforce, *Inquiry*, p. 91, on the principle that the authority of the Church's officers depends on their unanimity.
32 Boethius, *De Hebdomadibus*, ed. H.F. Stewart and E.K. Rand (London, 1973), p. 40.
33 Greenslade, op. cit., pp. 101, 108.

retrospective ratification through subsequent assent by the faithful,[34] when he asks 'what moved the faithful to refuse the second [Council] of Ephesus and willingly embrace the Council of Chalcedon?' He answers in terms of 'examining their decrees by Scripture'.[35] Hooker comes closer to the 'consensus and reception' principle in his notion that reason is to be used by the Christian as an instrument on which to test his growing understanding of the truth.[36] Henry Hammond among other seventeenth century authors explored this idea of 'right reason' as 'appointed ... judge of controversies'.[37] This operation of reason does not alter anything; it is not a creating of truth or a legitimizing of a decision. It is a process of recognition of a truth which already exists.

Christian consensus is corporate in a sense beyond what Cicero envisaged in remarking that what all peoples accept is natural law.[38] Hincmar of Rheims in the ninth century sees it as a sign of the unity of the Church that there should be consent and *consonantia*.[39] Erasmus in the sixteenth century thinks it wrong to dissent from the *sententia consensuque Ecclesiae*, the Church's agreed view.[40] We can thus see this authority in matters of faith as both a divine gift, God's own authority, and at the same time a function of communication among Christians, a living interplay in which there is perpetual mutual correction and room for growth in understanding.[41] That means that the growth of individual and corporate understanding, rather than the creation of truth, is the 'effect' of consensus. Consensus operates both intellectually, in 'judgement', and spiritually, in an embracing of the truth discovered.

The nature of Christian authority is thus such that it 'involves' rather than 'imposing on' minds and hearts. The notion of reception as an active welcoming rather than a passive acquiescence is adumbrated in the Middle Ages. The conception of active 'receiving' is put forward in the eleventh century by Anselm of Canterbury. In his *De Casu Diaboli* he tries to answer the question how some angels were able to persevere in righteousness while others were not. If God gave some perseverance and not others, it would seem that he condemned some to fall and that would

34 Chadwick, 'The status', p. 395.
35 Calfhill, PS, p. 155 f, 10 f. (writing in 1565).
36 See J.E. Booty, 'The judicious Mr. Hooker', Sykes, pp. 94-118.
37 Hammond, p. 29, cf. Waterland, p. 87.
38 K. Oehler, 'Der Consensus Omnium', *Antike und Abendlande*, 10 (1961), pp. 103-29. Cf. Y. Congar, 'Quod omnes tangit', *Revue historique de droit français et étranger* 66 (1958), pp. 210-59.
39 Ibid.
40 Thomas More, *Responsio ad Lutherum*, ed. J.M. Headley (London, 1969), V.198.27; Erasmus, *Epistolae*, ed. P.S. and H.M. Allen (Oxford, 1906-58), 6.206.
41 B-R, in Growth, p. 136.

make him the author of evil.   Anselm's explanation is that God gave
perseverance to them all, but only some accepted it; that is, it was by their
own active response that they received it.[42]   Although the word 'receive'
was in use in the sixteenth century in the general area of what we should
now call 'reception',[43] it was not yet an established technical term.   But the
notion of an active 'embracing' is clearly present.   'In general councils,
whatsoever is agreeable unto the written word of God we do reverently
embrace.'[44] 'Whatsoever is also grounded upon God's written word, though
not by our common and vulgar terms to be read therein, we do reverently
embrace.'[45] 'We must not only hear and understand ... but also with
steadfast assent of mind embrace ..., heartily love, ... yield ourselves
desirous and apt to learn, and to frame our minds to obey.'[46]

   The essence of this active welcoming is that it is not an individual but a
collective act of the people of God.   It shifts the emphasis of the word
consensus from its use in, for example, Aquinas, where it is merely an
agreement of the will to sin or to marriage, and so on, to the idea of shared
understanding: *consensus*.   Thus Melanchthon is able to define the Church
as: *homines amplectente Evangelium*,[47] people embracing the Gospel.   In the
same spirit the Thirty-Nine Articles urge that the Creeds 'ought *thoroughly*
to be received and believed'.   So reception is a response, and active response
of the people of God, not a 'passive acquiescence' or 'the submission of
obedience to a duly constituted authority'.[48]   It is both intellectual ('an active
exercise of the judgement') and 'a consent of the believing mind and
heart'.[49]   It is also a recognition, acting upon the community and not upon
the faith.   That is to say, it 'does not create truth or legitimise the decision.
It is the final indication that such a decision has fulfilled the necessary
conditions for it to be a true expression of the faith'.[50]   At the same time, it
acts upon the community to form the common mind.   'By reception we
mean the fact that the people of God acknowledge ... a decision or statement
because they recognise in it the apostolic faith.   They accept it because they
discern a harmony between what is proposed to them and the *sensus*

42 Anselm, *De Casu Diaboli*, 2-3, *Opera Omnia*, ed. F.S. Schmitt (Rome/Edinburgh,
    1938), I.235 ff.
43 More, Campbell, p. 111; Rogers, PS, p. 198; Cardwell, Synodalia II.492.
44 Rogers, PS, pp. 210-11.
45 Ibid., p. 201.
46 Nowell, PS, p. 117.
47 CR 24.401, cf. 406 and 409.
48 Proceedings of the General Synod of the Church of England, February, 1985, p. 75.
49 Ibid. Even though not everyone can be expected to judge theological technicalities, all
    can judge whether a doctrine as explained in non-technical terms corresponds with their
    own faith.
50 ARCIC A I, Elucidation 3.

fidelium of the whole Church'.[51] The voice of the Holy Spirit is being heard. 'Through that definition, whether it was of a synod or a primate, the authentic living voice of faith has been spoken in the Church, to the Church of God, by God.'[52] And that of course will be consonant with Scripture. It does not matter, then, what is the immediate source of the words or formula proposed. Whether conciliar, primatial or deriving from a committee or a commission or even an individual, they stand before the Church for reception. That receiving is a real 'testing', and it has a positive, vital effect in the forming of the common mind. This is the pattern of the living continuous process which goes on in the Church in tension with that which is eternal and unchanging in Christian truth as God has given it.

The structures in use at any given time in the Church's decision-making may reflect a variety of local customs and may take many forms.[53] The only things which are essential are the balance between the exercise of the ministry of oversight and the active involvement of the whole community,[54] and the understanding that divine authority flows perpetually through and within the body of the faithful. Thus we may say that the community speaks all the time collegially and from time to time through Councils and synods.[55] Stillness and growth, order and liberty, specially responsibilities and universal participation are held together by the Holy Spirit in living and challenging paradox, in which the essence is a shared or co-responsibility.

Guardianship of the faith

It has always been one of the pastoral authorities of bishops, entrusted to them as necessary for the effective discharge of their office of oversight, that they should teach the faith through the proclamation and explanation of the Word. This collective responsibility is there even when bishops are not assembled in Council, but acting in their own communities. In earlier centuries a bishop's local ministry of the Word was indispensable. In Augustine's day, and a century and a half later in the time of Gregory the Great, the bishop preached, applying Scripture to his people's spiritual and moral needs and seeking to show then what it reveals of the divine nature, God's work and God's promise. Alongside that continuing task there has grown up a critical scholarship which, from the rise of the universities in the twelfth century, has lain increasingly in the hands of academic theologians. (Some of these have, of course, subsequently become bishops.)

---

51 Proceedings of the General Synod, February, 1985, p. 75.
52 ARCIC A I, Elucidation 3. We may say that this has occurred in the case of the Creeds.
53 Cf. Suenens, *Dossier*, p. 71.
54 Ibid., p. 16.
55 See Newman, 'On consulting the faithfull'.

During the later mediaeval period critical work followed broadly the lines of the patristic view that every apparent anomaly or contradiction in the text of the Bible was there for a reason, a way in which the Holy Spirit came down to our level as sinners, and as creatures of limited understanding, to challenge us and to help our spiritual and intellectual growth. But new work on Greek and Hebrew was already beginning to suggest that some at least of these oddities in the text were the result of corruptions in its transmission, and from the sixteenth century something closer to the modern conception of critical scholarship began to emerge. In the last two hundred years a willingness to treat the Bible for academic purposes like any other ancient text, to apply to it the criteria of the historian and the scientist, has sometimes produced crises of popular confidence. And in recent decades the availability of modern media communication means that the bishop does not speak in such crises only to his own local congregations. It is the bishop's task here to seek, with his fellow-bishops, to help the community to see the importance of the continuing story of the Bible's preservation and of the unfolding of its teaching in each generation, to set new scholarly insights in the full context of Scripture's living witness, and to keep a sense of perspective about what seems new, in the light of a knowledge of the past. The 'challenge' of science or of philosophy, of logic or linguistics, has arisen in every century in the terms of the day; and it is an important aspect of the feeding of his sheep that the bishop should preserve from an anxiety which may seem to threaten their faith, those who have no means of assessing the superficially sometimes negative implications of what modern scholarship may seem to be saying about the fundamentals of Christian belief. The bishop seeks ways of involving the whole community in the forming of a common mind, and making the understanding of the past contemporary, a living appreciation of the lively Word.

We have been speaking of 'decision-making'. That cannot be quite the right term for a process which does not create truth or legitimise decisions but only appropriates a truth which is already there. But it can have reference to the question of 'binding' the community which so exercised the minds of those involved in bringing together the first Lambeth Conferences. It also bears on the question of the inerrancy of Councils or Papal pronouncements which remains a stumbling-block for some protestants.

The 1922 Doctrine Commission suggested that since 'the authority of the Church in the realm of doctrine arises from its commission to preach the Gospel to all the world', we may rely on 'the promises, accompanying that commission, that the Lord would always be with his disciples, and that the

Holy Spirit would guide them into all the truth'.[56] In answer to the
question, 'Why, then, does the Holy Spirit allow imperfect consensus,
periods of learning from our mistakes, and so slow a growth in
understanding?', we must answer that in the deep structures of decision-
making our human needs and failings are accepted and allowed for, and the
mode of our learning together is in tune with the enabling of our growth in
holiness through living together in the faith. If God never forces his
people's consent it must follow that 'the Spirit's guidance is not irresistible
and that the Church in history has not necessarily at all points been perfectly
responsive to its infallible guide'.

At times in the course of the process of discovery of the fullness of truth
in which we are still engaged, there have been major crises: for example
over the Arians in the fourth century. In such circumstances there has
proved to be a special task for the ministry of oversight, acting directly and
decisively in emergency. Wollebius, who published a Reformed
Compendium of Christian theology in 1626, sees the twofold pattern thus:
the fundamental process of decision-making by judgement and 'embracing'
goes on in the community as a whole. 'Doctrine can and ought to be
examined by all,' he says, including lay people,' to see whether it agrees
with Scripture'. But he imputes to those with a ministry of oversight a
responsibility for dealing with 'the more serious crises' and taking
emergency action when fundamentals are in question. This is a special
exercise of the underlying and continuing responsibility for the
guardianship of the faith, borne by the Church as a whole and focused as a
matter of order in the leaders of the community. If this is right, and the
office of oversight as we have described it, the implication would seem to be
that when fundamental matters of faith are in question, the Church can make
judgements, consonant with Scripture, which are authoritative, and that in
such emergency conditions these will normally need to be made by those
with a responsibility for oversight for practical reasons of urgency and
rapid communicability, and also as carrying an immediate and binding
though provisional authority. We need to be clear what this means.

Such a judgement must satisfy rigorous conditions. It must be consonant
with Scripture. It must share the characteristic of all right decisions in
matters of faith, in clarifying the truth, not adding to it. It must be made,
whether by a primate or by a council of bishops, with the intention that it be
a statement of the whole fellowship. That means that such a pronouncement
is made focally and representatively for the whole community, and remains
ultimately to be received by the whole community. It must be made without
duress (for example, political pressure), with the intention of issuing a

---

[56] Report of the Doctrine Commission (1922), (London, 1938), p. 35.

decision on a matter of faith or morals which the mind of the Church will
be able to recognise. Where it is a primatial judgement, it must be made
after consultation with the primate's fellow-bishops, and in accordance with
their consensus. Thus a primatial initiative taken in conditions of
emergency is in intention and in fact a collegial statement, expressing the
mind of the Church as articulated by those with the responsibility of
oversight, and made by a primate on that understanding.[57] These are all
indications that it is being made under the guidance of the Holy Spirit.

When all these conditions are fulfilled (and this will sometimes become
clear only over time), the truth expressed in the definition may be taken to
be free from error and to have been arrived at under the guidance of the
Holy Spirit. That does not mean that the definition cannot be perfected or
made complete; or that it cannot be restated subsequently. It is, of its
essence, an emergency statement, and as such has force as what we may call
a 'working consensus'. But because it carries the ordinary inherent
authority of those to whom the ministry of oversight has been entrusted, it
is decisive for the emergency situation. Melanchthon suggested during the
Lutheran debates that obedience is due in the same way to a decision arrived
at through the Church's structures of decision-making rightly used in this
way, as to any right understanding of Scripture. 'When a pronouncement is
made according to a right understanding of the Word of God, it is necessary
for everyone to obey it, just as certain holy Councils have pronounced on
various controversies.'[58] William Laud, too, speaks of 'obedience' in such a
context.[59] We may see this 'obedience' as a commiting of the community to
the truth thus expressed, on the understanding that it may come to be more
fully grasped and more exactly expressed as a result of its receiving by the
whole people of God. That is the manner in which it is immediate and
binding, and at the same time provisional, as expressing a truth free from
error in the most exact language which can be framed at the time.

But the full operation of these processes requires a united Church. In the
present divided state of the universal Church they can proceed only
imperfectly. Further division, which would further hamper their working,
is still sometimes threatened under pressure of controversy. There is an
imperative need to arrive at a means of provisional decision-making in the
separated communions which will both strengthen their internal unity, and
foster the cause of unity in the universal Church.

[57] Cf. ARCIC, Authority II, 29.
[58] Melanchthon on the Council of Ratisbon, 1541, CR, 4.352.
[59] Laud, *Fisher*, pp. 62-3.

'Confessional' formularies

This brings us again to the notion of 'confessional identity' and the related question of what a Communion or a Province may do or decide on its own account in the present divided Church, without further prejudice to the unity of the body of Christ. The sixteenth century Articles of the Church of England endorse the view that such 'traditions' as rites and ceremonies are at the disposal of the Church in different places to decree as appropriate to local needs (Article 33 of 1552, 34 of 1571). The articles say that these must meet two tests. The first is conformity with Scripture, and the second that they should be established locally by common authority (*publica auctoritas*). The Articles argue that such ruling ought to be obeyed in these circumstances in deference to that authority, and so as to avoid troubling the consciences of weaker brethren (*ibid.*). They are obeyed, in other words, for the preservation of order, conceived of in terms of obedience and mutual respect.

But this was not, even in the sixteenth century, a straightforward matter of variation in the forms of services. Liturgy is also theology. The debate about 'rites' was set on foot by the reformers because they believed that the Church was teaching the people theological errors through its rites (especially in the penitential system and in encouraging the veneration of images, for example). The claim to vary rites and ceremonies locally was thus also in some measure a claim to authority locally in deciding matters of faith. William Beveridge (1637-1708) picks out 'two things' as belonging in some autonomously determinable way to a Church's authority: 'the decreeing of ceremonies' and 'the determining of controversies'.[60] The matter is further compounded by the legitimate existence both of traditions which are 'customs of the Church produced by the frequent and long-continued usage of the great part of the community' and which are rightly precious to that group of Christians; and also of traditions of the Church universal, that is, of the whole community over time. So long as it is without prejudice to theological consensus, there must be room for variety in practice. The difficulty is to define the limits of that variation which must operate if there is not to be a consequent division in matters of faith. T.I. Ball summed up the problem neatly in 1877. Both matters of 'practice' and matters of 'doctrine' as 'received in the Church' have been drawn out of 'the Church's written *depositum*, the Holy Scriptures'. But the extent of the Church's 'power over rites and ceremonies is very large indeed. The extent of the authority of the Church in controversies of faith ... is confined within very narrow limits'.

[60] Beveridge, *Ecclesia Anglicana*, p. 118.

Anglicans inherit in the sixteenth century Articles, liturgy and other formularies, a sixteenth century attempt to unite forms of worship with a common core of doctrine as a basis for confessional identity. The 'Articles, Liturgy, Creeds and Catechism', are described by Daniel Waterland (1683-1740) as 'our Church's forms' and he wrote in some anxiety about the way any attempt at innovation or change should be judged. ('Let both be tried by the Scripture-rule, to see whether the new or old be better').[61] John Owen was suspicious of the claim of any Church to be a Church on the basis of 'a peculiar form of its own'.[62] But in general there has been strong loyalty among Anglicans, at least until comparatively recent times, to the sixteenth century formularies and to the liturgy which embodies much Anglican theology. The 1867 Lambeth Conference was concerned to limit experimentation with the liturgy by provision that 'all alterations in the Services of the Church, required by circumstances in the Province should be made or authorised by the Provincial Synod, not merely by the Diocesan'.[63] The Conferences of 1878[64] and of 1888[65] signalled the dangers to doctrinal consensus of careless liturgical change. The Thirty-Nine Articles have continued to be a formulary to which ordained ministers must subscribe, but there has been heated debate, particularly during the nineteenth century,[66] about their intention, enduring validity and modern relevance (and the not unimportant question whether a subscription to the English formularies made on the principle for 'private judgement' is in fact compatible with the very recognition of Church authority which it is intended to imply).[67]

There have been several attempts since the framing of the Thirty-Nine Articles to set out what is basic to the faith. The notion of a hierarchy of truths, some not 'necessary to salvation' was already current in the late Middle Ages. It needs handling with care, as seventeenth and eighteenth century Anglican divines discovered in attempts to identify 'fundamentals'. It cannot be right to suggest that the province of authorising in divided

61 *Remarks*, p. 4.
62 *Of Schism*, pp. 188-9. See Resp. 219, on 'forms'.
63 1867, p. 61.
64 1878, pp. 86, 89.
65 1888, p. 152.
66 For example, Goode, op. cit. and the debate about Tract 90. The Lambeth Conference of 1888 comments that the Thirty-Nine Articles are 'statements of doctine, for the most part accurate in their language and reserved and moderate in their definitions ... the Articles are not all of equal value ... they are not, and do not profess to be, a complete statement of Christian doctrine ... From the temporary and local circumstances under which they were composed, they do not always meet the requirements of Churches formed under wholly different conditions' (Lambeth, 1888, p. 174). On formal procedures for liturgical change, see *Church and State*, Chapter 2.
67 Wilberforce, *Inquiry*, p. 212.

Communions is limited to matters low in the 'hierarchy of truths'. Each such Communion affirms its catholicity by joining with the whole Church in authorising the great central truths of faith. But, as William Laud put it, the Church of England 'is not such a shrew to her children as to deny her blessing, or denounce an anathema against them, if some peaceably dissent in some particulars remoter from the foundation'.[68] It has been an Anglican habit to speak of 'comprehensiveness' and to identify as characteristically Anglican the pursuing of 'a middle way, not as a compromise, but as a positive grasp of many-sided truth'. This is seen by the Lambeth Conference of 1968 as a 'richness' enabling Anglicans 'to live, both in fellowship and in tension, with those who in some points differ from us'.[69] Nevertheless, 'a limit ... there must be to freedom of opinion within a communion which possesses a definite creed'.[70] Comprehensiveness must have definable bounds. There is a question of the limits of tolerance to be extended to those who would share 'external communion'. Here the apparently peripheral may prove to be more central than it seemed. In Richard Baxter's seventeenth century defence of various Anglican practices and principles there is much behind. (Godfathers and Godmothers, the people bearing a part in the Responses, kneeling at the Sacrament, the use of the sign of the Cross in baptism, for example.)[71] The lesson would seem to be that it is important not to try to distinguish central truths for universal agreement and leave the rest to local licence, but to seek a consensus on all matters, which embraces the full range of understanding represented in variations of local practice and emphasis.

Nor can it be right to make other sources such as confessional formularies fixed standards in the same way as Scripture. The 1922 Doctrine Commission says that the Anglican Formularies, for example, 'should not be held to prejudge questions which have arisen since their formulation, or problems which have been modified by fresh knowledge or fresh conceptions'.[72] We must, therefore, if we are to use the term 'standards', work with some sense of the terms which allows for restatement and growth in a living community. It is easy to see that process at work in

---

68 Laud, *Fisher*, pp. 59-60.
69 Lambeth, 1968, p. 141.
70 J.B. Mozley, Subscription to the Articles (Oxford, 1863), p. 32. Compare W. Goode, *Tract XC Historically Refuted* (London, 1845) on the notion that the Articles were originally propounded in 'a vague indecisive and therefore comprehensive sense', p. 5.
71 Richard Baxter, *Vindication of the Church of England* (London, 1682), defends standing up at the Creed and Antiphons, Episcopal Confirmation, organ music in church, Godfather and Godmothers, the people bearing a part in the Responses, bowing at the name of Jesus, the oaths taken by priests and deacons of canonical obedience to their diocesan, surplices, and a number of other matters.
72 *Report* of the Doctrine Commission (1922) (London, 1938), p. 37.

the history of Anglican reflection on the Thirty-Nine Articles. Richard Hooker (c. 1554-1600) put forward his trio of Scripture, tradition and reason in the context of contemporary debate about the need for any guide at all but Scripture. Others in the seventeenth century were chiefly anxious to differentiate the Thirty-Nine Articles from 'the doctrine of those commonly called Presbyterians' on the one side, and the tenets of the Church of Rome on the other because they saw that as the way to stress something which is distinctively and constitutively Anglican. It is a mark of ecumenical progress that that now seems to many a false goal and the wrong way to go about it. William Beveridge in 1710 had the idea of 'consonance' in wanting to show that the Articles were 'consonant to Scripture, reason and the Fathers'. Henry Cary in 1835 supplied 'Testimonies of the Fathers of the first four centuries to the doctrine and discipline of the Church of England as set forth in the Thirty-Nine articles', in an endeavour to show the continuity of the Church of England with the early Church. Richard Bentley Porson Kidd listed 'testimonies and authorities, divine and human' in confirmation of the Articles (1848), Joseph Miller (1878-87), E. Tyrrell Green (1896), B.J. Kidd (1899), W. Goode (1845), placed an emphasis upon the witness of history.

If we may take it, then, that life and worship in the Church, though locally variable, are ultimately inseparable from questions of unity of faith with the whole believing community of the universal Church; that 'fundamentals' cannot be separated from the fullness of Christian believing; that the truth once for all delivered (and thus 'standard'), is also maintained and living and growing in the Church; we can begin to set in context the question of a characteristically 'Anglican' faith. The Lambeth Quadrilateral of 1888 lists Scripture, the Creeds, the Sacraments and the historic Episcopate[73] as the four standards. The intention was ecumenical. That is to say, it was envisaged that upon these four fundamentals a future united Church might be constructed. Nevertheless, the Conference of 1888 distinguished between 'the standard of doctrine of the Universal Church which the whole Anglican Communion has always accepted' and 'those which are especially the heritage of the Church of England, and which are, to a greater or less extent, received by all her sister and daughter Churches'. These are listed as the sixteenth century formularies, 'The Prayer Book with its Catechism, the Ordinal, and the Thirty-Nine Articles of Religion'. It is the position of documents which claim to be the special source or standard for a particular ecclesial body, as distinct from a valued part of its heritage

---

[73] See *Quadrilateral at One Hundred*, ed. J. Robert Wright (Ohio, London and Oxford, 1988) for a recent series of essays.

or tradition, with which we have been concerned here, because it raises the question of their status.

The Lambeth Quadrilateral speaks of 'articles', but the Chicago version of 1886 which served as its model describes its clauses as 'inherent parts of this sacred deposit'. The word 'parts' undoubtedly fits the grammatical form and the meaning of the Quadrilateral clauses better. In neither the Chicago nor the Lambeth version are they strictly 'clauses' at all; there is no verb. The focus is actually upon a series of things: Scripture, the Creeds, the Sacraments, the historic Episcopate. In each case the noun is qualified by a phrase explaining how it is to be understood (the Creeds 'as the sufficient statement of the Christian faith', for example). This is not a point of pedantry; the difference is crucial. Of one of the Thirty-Nine Articles I may say, 'I believe that ...', and make by quoting it a propositional statement of a doctrinal position on the issue in question. Of one of the clauses of the Lambeth Quadrilateral I must say, 'I believe in ...'. So, in the Quadrilateral's clauses we have something much like the sixteenth century 'notes of the Church', or their ancient equivalents, four things which when present are taken to indicate that we have a 'true Church'. As the Lambeth Quadrilateral sees it, it is a living community within which Scripture is active, underpinning the Creeds, ministered in the sacraments, guarded and preached under the oversight of the episcopate. With a slightly different emphasis in mind, the 1922 Doctrine Commission lists Scripture, the Church, the Creeds and the Anglican Formularies. Here Scripture is taken as the bedrock of revelation, which keeps authenticating itself by 'continuing to mediate to individuals the revelation which it records and by nurturing their spiritual life'. But again it is being seen in the context of the life of the believing community of the Church and in harness with the Creeds.[74] The key difference - and it is of great importance - is the emphasis on the Anglican Formularies as defining 'the position of the Church of England in relation to other Christian bodies'.[75] That strikes a disjunctive note deliberately omitted from the Lambeth Quadrilateral, and surely out of tune with its central ecumenical purpose.[76]

Yet there must be proper spheres of authorising within the Anglican, or any other Communion, and arguably within provinces. If Beveridge is right, it is the place of each ecclesial body to word the truths of faith which belong to and are apprehended by the community of the universal Church, in ways comfortable and natural and appropriate to the style and character of the individual Communion, and which may be used in its life and

[74] *Report* of the Doctrine Commission (1922) (London, 1938), p. 31.
[75] Ibid., p. 36.
[76] G.R. Evans, 'Permanence in the Revealed Truth and Continuous Exploration of its Meaning', *Quadrilateral at One Hundred*, pp. 111 ff.

worship, but always with care not inadvertently to set up a barrier to other Christians. It is also the duty of each body to correct error and misunderstanding in its midst, and to work always towards unanimity with the *consensus fidelium*. We must therefore carefully separate a sense of corporate identity based on common norms of worship and on common life within a Communion, from the expectation that Anglicans will share a common faith which somehow distinguishes them from other Christians. That cannot be right. Everything we know about faith endorses the view that it unite us to the whole Body of Christ's faithful people through Christ, and is thus a corporate believing with the universal community. Matters of doctrine are always the responsibility of the universal Church and never at the disposal of a local community without reference to the whole under Scripture.

All this has implications for authorising in matters of faith and practice within individual provinces; and within the particular churches, or individual dioceses; and, with certain restrictions, for individual congregations, insofar as these may be deemed ecclesial bodies. An ecclesial community may, within the limits set by orderliness, legislate for its own people. It may do so freely in matters which cannot be divisive in relation to other communions or communities, provided its actions are consonant with Scripture, causing no difficulty to tender consciences. In all matters of faith and worship where there is known to be imperfect consensus as yet in the universal Church the diocese or province or communion must be prepared in charity to 'defer to the common mind'. That may mean being patient until all can agree. It may mean seeking to lead the common mind into agreement. There should never be any attempt to force others into conformity with a *fait accompli*. In practice such precipitate action has sometimes been taken, and situations created in which some are unable in conscience to accept the resulting position as compatible with universal faith and order. Here again the rule of charity operates. No communion, provinces or diocese should respond in anger, or in any manner likely to lead to division. Solutions must be sought which reconcile and foster the growth of common life. Where this purpose is paramount, and anger and resentment not allowed to confuse the real issues, we may go on in faith that the Lord, whose intention for his Church is that it should be one with him, will bring about a right resolution of differences. Deference to the common mind means a willingness to accept that one may be wrong and to grow in understanding, as well as a pooling of the Communion's special insights into the fullness of the truth.

Chapter Nine

Authority in moral matters

> The positive nature of the authority which binds the Anglican
> Communion together is ... seen to be moral and spiritual, resting
> on the truth of the Gospel, and on a charity which is patient and
> willing to defer to the common mind.[1]

We must get clear at the outset the equivocal character of recent Anglican
usage of the term 'moral authority'. When, in a series of statements, the
Lambeth Conferences outlined what they took to be a characteristically
Anglican conception here, they were not referring specifically to authority
in moral matters, but to the general tone or style of Anglican authorising.[2]
In 1867 we find the notion of an authority derived 'from the moral weight
of ... united counsels and judgements' and 'from the voluntary acceptance of
its conclusions by any of the Churches there represented'.[3] An authority
which 'does not claim to exercise any powers of control or command' is
seen as standing for 'the far more spiritual and more Christian principle of
loyalty to the fellowship', a fellowship in which the Churches 'are indeed
independent, but independent with the Christian freedom which recognises
the restraints of truth and of love'; thus the Churches 'are not free to deny
the truth' and 'they are not free to ignore the fellowship'.[4] The 1948
Committee Report sets this style of authorising by 'moral authority' over
against 'centralised government' and 'a legal basis of union'. Its tone is
patent in the Lambeth texts; there is no giving of orders. 'We utter an
emphatic warning' (Resolution 68, 1920); 'we desire solemnly to commend
... to all who will hear' (ibid.); 'The Conference presses' (Resolution 71,
1920); 'the Conference ... urges' (Resolution 72, 1920). It has to be frankly
admitted that this kind of emphasis reflects a deliberate wish on the part of
the bishops who made up these Conferences to distance their way of
proceeding from what was seen as the Roman Catholic way.[5] That, as we

---

[1] Lambeth, 1948, p. 84.
[2] That is, to a definition of 'moral' which refers to a kind of proof which falls short of
being demonstrative, as when we speak of something being 'morally certain'.
[3] Lambeth, 1867, p. 62.
[4] Encyclical Letter, Lambeth Conference, 19.
[5] For instance, the Supreme Congregation of the Holy Office in an Instruction of 1956 on
'Situation Ethics' 'forbids ...'. For an instance of Anglican hostility, see Lambeth, 1897

shall see, was disingenuous in view of the earlier Anglican heritage of a model of authority which was far from 'moral' in this sense, and on occasion coercive to the point of making martyrs.[6]

It is against this background of a relatively modern conception of 'moral authority' in Anglicanism that we must set the related but subordinate question of authority in moral matters. The Report of the 1978 Lambeth Conference lists among the 'different forms of authority' with which a bishop works, a 'moral authority'.[7] This is in part a matter of setting a personal example. 'The Christ-like life carries its own authority'.[8] But it is also a recognition that the bishop's 'superintendence', his disciplinary role and his central ministry of reconciliation as president of the eucharistic community, come together in early, patristic and mediaeval tradition most conspicuously in the exercise of 'the power of the keys'. This is consistently seen in patristic and mediaeval tradition as a commission from Christ to decide points in dispute as well as to give rulings concerning the position of individuals who err. It was in line with the understanding that the bishop is the person who acts on behalf of the community in admitting to membership, that in the serious instances of lapse into sin (murder, adultery, apostasy) in the early Church, the bishops pronounced a sentence of excommunication on behalf of the community; this was simply an exclusion from Communion. The readmission of penitents was also a public act of the whole community, and it symbolised a return not only to a state of forgiveness before God, but also to the community of Christ's body. Cyprian says that the final decision to restore the penitent must be in the bishop's hands, but that he must be advised by his presbyters and the 'confessors', and act before the congregation.

Discipline

In the mediaeval period the episcopal role was still important in the case of serious offences. In the penitential canons of 963 in England we find the instruction that every bishop shall be in his episcopal chair on Ash Wednesday to hear penitents 'defiled with capital crimes'.[9] Lanfranc, as Archbishop of Canterbury in 1072, similarly restricted serious crimes to

Committee on Church Unity, which wanted to refuse a 'condition of complete submission on our part to those claims of absolute authority ... against which we have been for three centuries bound to protest'.

6 The sixteenth century record is clear here.
7 Lambeth, 1978, p. 76.
8 1948, Lambeth Conference Report on the Anglican Communion.
9 Johnson I.431. (Johnson, 1662-75, collected early English sources, in *Works* (1847).)

episcopal jurisdiction.[10] The notion of a satisfaction made to the community presented in general no problems to the reformers of the sixteenth century.[11] Article 33 of the Thirty-Nine Articles endorses the need for the excommunicated to the 'openly reconciled' and 'received in the Church by a Judge that hath authority thereunto'. The mediaeval extension of the public penalty which meant that sometimes excommunication was used as a political sanction to bring recalcitrant princes to heel, or to strike fear into ordinary people if they did not pay their taxes, was another matter. That seemed to the reformers an abuse of disciplinary power in the Church.[12]

The change from a general system of 'public' penance to a 'private' pattern had enormous ramifications. At the end of the fourth century in the West there was a move from baptism in adulthood and often late in life, to infant baptism. That meant that it became unlikely that anyone would go through life without committing some relatively serious sin after baptism. The provision for dealing with penitents had to be modified, to meet the need for a more or less routine and repeated repentance throughout the community. By Carolingian times this universal pastoral need was being met locally by private confession to a priest, who imposed a penance laid down according to a scale used throughout the region, so that everyone might be treated equally. Such penitential canons were often ratified by kings[13] but in intention they were the provisions of bishops, who were thus continuing to oversee the system juridically, even though what passed between penitent and confessor was a private and not a public matter, and pressure of need made it impossible for the bishop to hear all penitents himself, or to pronounce absolution personally in every case.[14] By the time of the Lateran Council of 1215, every Christian was obliged to confess his sins to a priest before coming to the Eucharist, on the understanding that unless he did so, received absolution and carried out the penitential acts

---

10 Lanfranc, *Constitutions*, 1072, Johnson II.9.

11 Melanchthon understood that the prime purpose of the penitential system in the early Church had not been to make possible satisfaction of a God who already knew the penitent's heart, but to satisfy the community of the sincerity of repentance (*Apologia* for the Augsburg Confession Article 12, Tappert, p. 199). Calvin also explains that the Fathers understood satisfaction as made to the community, and he castigates the 'schoolmen' for misreading patristic authority on this point, *Institutes* III.iv.39).

12 Cf. Luther, Sermon on the Ban, 1520, and Calvin, *Antidote* to the Paris Articles of 1544, CR 35.33-4.

13 Johnson found some pre-Conquest English examples.

14 In Peter Lombard's *Sentences* it is noted that the keys are given to a priest at his ordination *per ministerium episcopi* IV, Dist. 19.1.

enjoined on him, he could not be 'in communion'.[15] In the rubric which precedes the Book of Common Prayer order of service for Holy Communion we find the direction that if the local minister has reason to believe that someone who presents himself to be a 'partaker of Holy Communion' is in breach of charity with his neighbours, or in some 'grave and open sin without repentance', he shall give an account of the matter to his bishop, and under the bishop's direction may refuse him the sacrament. Anglican authors have maintained for the most part the position that only a bishop or priest may declare Christ's forgiveness to the penitent, and Anglican liturgy enshrines the principle in practice.

The conception of 'judgement' embodied here has sometimes been seen as declarative only, sometimes as also judicial in Anglican writings. The sixteenth century liturgy is ambivalent on the point. In the absolution in the Eucharist the priest says (or the bishop if he is present, whether or not he is the celebrant), 'Almighty God ... have mercy upon you ... etc.' Hickes (1642-1715) thought it 'plain that the Christians of the second century looked upon the censured sinner as precondemned by God; and [took it] that the sentence of excommunication, and by consequence of absolution, was not only declarative but judicial'.[16] Luther and Melanchthon agree that when the words of absolution are spoken, it has the same significance as if Christ himself passed judgement, and that we must believe the voice of one absolving as we should believe a voice coming from heaven. The influence of contemporary debates prompted the framers of the Book of Common Prayer to include an emphasis upon the 'comforting of the terrified conscience', as Lutheran tradition puts it.[17] This is found in the exhortation to be given when the minister announces the day of a forthcoming celebration of Holy Communion:

> If any of you ... cannot quiet his own conscience, but requireth further comfort or counsel, let him come to me, or to some other discreet and learned Minister of God's Word, and open his grief; that by the ministry of God's holy Word he may receive the benefit of absolution, together with ghostly counsel and advice.

Here the sacramental ministry is seen in the Lutheran way as deriving from

---

15 'A priest ought not to reconcile a penitent without consulting his bishop, unless ultimate necessity forces him to do so', says Peter Lombard, citing the second Council of Carthage (*Sentences* IV, Dist. 19.6).

16 Hickes, *Two Treatises on Christian Priesthood*, p. 159.

17 The 'judgemental' responsibility of the ordained minister should be seen as a responsibility not to issue pardon mechanically, although this was a common practice in the Middle Ages, and many exhortations to confessors were issued to try to improve matters.

and mediated by the ministry of the Word; it is of importance that the comfort of the conscience is linked here with absolution.[18]

The sixteenth century Church of England retained a canon law whose origins are far older than the refinements (and corruptions) of the penitential system to which the reformers objected in the practice of the late mediaeval Church. Although the equipage of the penitential system was largely discarded in sixteenth century England, the Canons settled on in 1604 provided comprehensive legal sanctions in moral matters. Something had to be done to make up for one's offences. It was intended that 'notorious crimes: adultery, whoredom, incest, drunkenness, swearing, ribaldry, usury or any other uncleanness and wickedness of life' should be 'punished by the severity of the laws'.[19] The very exemplary character of the moral authority which bishops and other clergy ought to exercise is enshrined in law and sanctions provided for it. Ministers, 'having always in mind, that they ought to excel all others in purity of life, and should be examples to the people who live well and Christianly, do so under pain of ecclesiastical censures, to be inflicted with severity, according to the qualities of their offences'.[20]

There was no question in the minds of the framers of these canons that the community, through its officers, ought to exercise authority in moral matters, and an authority in which there is not only the attractiveness of good example, but the element of discipline for offenders, too.[21] Nor was it questioned that the community, through its officers, ought to exclude from the Eucharist those who were guilty of persistent and public offences: 'Notorious offenders ... openly known to live in sin notorious, without repentance', or who have offended against the law of charity which binds the community together ('who have maliciously and openly contended with their neighbours, until they shall be reconciled').[22] The same exclusion applies, *ipso facto*, to schismatics.[23] The underlying principles here were consciously those of the early Church, where the whole business of penance was a public matter.[24] But it cannot be said that the English reformers intended to restrict authority in moral matters to a community action, either through exclusion from Holy Communion or through the courts. There is

18 There is also a retention of the ancient principle that a penitent (under the system of private confession), may go to any minister.
19 1604 Canons, xcii ff. (in Cardwell, *Synodalia*).
20 1604 Canons, lxxv.
21 Not of course to be exercised without mercy.
22 1604 Canons, xxvi.
23 1604 Canons, xxvii.
24 See B. Poschmann, *Penance and the Anointing of the Sick* (Frieburg, 1967), tr. F. Courtenay.

abundant recognition in the Book of Common Prayer that a priest or bishop is entrusted personally with the power to bind and loose. In the ordination of a priest in the 1662 service we have, 'Whose sins thou dost forgive, they are forgiven; and whose sins thou dost retain, they are retained'. An absolution follows the General Confession at morning and evening prayer, as well as in the service of Holy Communion. In the debate of November, 1984 on 'The Reconciliation of a Penitent' in the General Synod of the Church of England, one speaker said in support of the view that the authority of the keys rests in this way with the priest or bishop: 'I am quite sure that there are very many souls who have not been able, either through preaching of the Word or through public declaration of God's absolution, to accept and receive their own release from the burden of guilt ... Many such people need to be told not that God forgives everyone ...; they need also to be told, 'You are forgiven'. 'The priest ... has the position of the soul bearing to the penitent the joy of freedom and forgiveness'.[25]

The relationship between this personal, and the community's, authority in matters of morals is a complex one in the Church's historical practice, and it brings us back to the general area of decision-making, but in its particular reference to discipline. We have said that in present-day understanding the bishop is the servant of the community but he may exercise discipline on its behalf in the interests of that order which is 'love in regulative operation.'[26] This authority is defined in modern English Canon Law in terms of the bishop's 'jurisdiction as ordinary' (Canon C 18.2). This ordinary inherent jurisdiction makes him 'principal minister' in his diocese and gives him the 'right' of 'summoning all synods and diocesan conferences and of presiding therein' (C 18.5). It also requires him to 'correct and punish all such as be unquiet, disobedient, or criminous, within his diocese, according to such authority as he has by God's Word and is committed to him by the laws and ordinances of this realm' (C 18.7). Church of England Canon Law says that 'the inferior clergy who have received authority to minister in any diocese owe canonical obedience ... to the bishop of the same' (C 3, C 14). This is essentially a legal power, and *mutatis mutandis*, is equivalent to the power of 'ordinary in law' exercised by a bishop in the Roman Catholic Church'.[27] But it is also rooted in the larger order of the Church, which embraces both the *ordo* of ordination and the *ordo* of structure. Because this ordinary inherent power is exercised within the community it is possible to speak of 'ordinary inherent power' in a synod, too.[28] Nevertheless, 'no resolution in

25 J. Pearce, *Proceedings* of the General Synod, 15 Nov. 1984, p. 1158.
26 A-R, 82.
27 Codex Iuris Canonici, 204, 208.
28 Lathbury, p. 477.

any ... synod or diocesan conference shall have effect without the sanction of the bishop', says modern English Canon Law, although that sanction 'is not lightly nor without grave cause to be withheld' (C 18.5). To that end the bishop 'exercises and works with' the whole complex of Christian authorities we have been examining, that of Scripture; that of tradition; moral authority; the authority of his office; the authority of counsel by scholars and experts.[29] This is a co-operative ministerial authorising resting on the principle of the equality in dignity of all the Christian faithful incorporated in Christ through baptism,[30] and it is one in which matters of morals and discipline cannot really be separated from the rest.

Similar principles of discipline and obedience, with legal sanction in and through the community, extend into Anglican provincial government. English Canon Law at present states that an archbishop has 'jurisdiction as ordinary' throughout his province, 'as superintendent of all ecclesiastical matters therein, to correct and supply the defects of other bishops' (C 17). As the 'clergy who have received authority to minister in any diocese owe canonical obedience ... to the bishop of the same' so the bishop of each diocese owes 'due allegiance to the archbishop of the province as his metropolitan' (C 3). This 'due allegiance' or 'due obedience' (C 14) is technically distinct from 'canonical obedience' in the language of Canon Law, because it is due among 'equals in the structure' of the Church's order to one bishop who acts as a focus and sometimes spokesman of the college of bishops. It implies an equality of all dioceses in a province and thus of all local or particular churches. The metropolitan see has, as a diocese, no pre-eminence among them. But the metropolitan or archbishop has a personal ordinary inherent jurisdiction derived from the submission of his fellow-bishops for the sake of preserving what we may call the regulative operation of love in the province. Thus during, and only during, the time of his metropolitan visitation, the archbishop has 'jurisdiction as Ordinary' (C 17). There are implications for a wider primacy. It has not been usual in recent Anglican Canon Law or practice to define at all fully the obligation of obedience which rests on the members of the community who are not ordained.

Moral decision-making

Formal consultative decision-making in matters of morals, with legislative purpose, takes place in synods in the modern Anglican Communion. One way of understanding the powers of decision-making which reside in

---

[29] Lambeth, 1978, p. 76.
[30] *Codex Iuris Canonici*, 204, 208.

councils and synods - though not one for which universal claims can be made - is in terms of 'legislative' power. The limits of such legislative power must be of two kinds. First, the law can make a crime but not a sin. That is to say, it can provide only legal not moral sanctions against certain actions.[31] The authority for moral choice does not lie in the legislative, judicial or executive powers of a bishop or synod, and still less in secular legislature, but derives from God alone. As Henry Hammond put it in the seventeenth century, 'For a thing to be morally good ... depends, by sure connection, from that eternal justice which is primarily in God'.[32] So any attempt by the state to legislate on moral questions runs into the difficulty that they are not susceptible of full definition and enforcement as civil offences because the ultimate issues of right and wrong involved go beyond the reach of legislation to frame or dispose of. So we are left with an authority in moral matters mediated through the Church, which cannot correspond exactly with legislative provision by the state, and ought not to do so, because, even if it were possible, that would be to reduce the consequences of sin to a problem manageable by the provisions of human society.

The second principle is that whatever legislative powers with reference to the Church reside in its authoritative structures, must be given some legislative extension by secular authority if they are to have force in society at large, and be endorsed there as right, customary and reliable. Every local church exists in a secular community and (without compromising with the truth) must govern its life in ways which are appropriate to the circumstances in which it finds itself.[33] Every Christian is also a citizen living under secular law. Throughout the later mediaeval centuries there was a running battle over the respective jurisdictions of secular and ecclesiastical courts, and over rights to temporalities, or Church holdings of lands and goods. The procedure of the English Church since the sixteenth century has been to submit canons made in Convocation (or latterly the General Synod), to Parliament and to Royal Assent, in order that both legislative systems may work in harness and in harmony.[34] In other provinces such legislative extension follows a variety of local patterns. It is always a matter for discussion how far moral or secular law should reach into private life.

All this rests on the understanding that human actions matter in the sight of God. The Thirty-Nine Articles concentrate upon those aspects of the

---

[31] Canons on 1969, Introduction. See Robert Ombres, 'Faith, Doctrine and Roman Catholic Law', in *Journal of the Ecclesiastical Law Society* (forthcoming).

[32] Hammond, p. 29.

[33] Cf. Guncdrum, p. 8.

[34] Canons of 1969, p. xi. See, too, *Church and State* on these procedures.

question of 'works' which were particularly contentious in the sixteenth century. They insist upon the helplessness of man to do good works without the aid of grace (Article 10); that good works which are the fruits of faith are 'pleasing and acceptable to God in Christ' (Article 12); that works, though objectively speaking they may be 'good', are not pleasing to God if they are not done in conscious faithful obedience to the direction of the Holy Spirit (the controversial Article 13). Such concerns have still been well to the force in twentieth century conversations. In a Conference between the Church of England and the Church of Finland in 1933-4, for example, it was argued that 'man must be saved in order to do good works', not the opposite: 'Man must do good works in order to be saved', and that in the latter case Christianity would be 'degraded to the level of mere morality'.[35] In a further Conference between the Church of England and the Evangelical Lutheran Churches of Latvia and Estonia in 1938 the twelfth Article of the Augsburg Confession of 1530 with its insistence that good works are 'fruits of repentance' was seen as fundamental by the Lutherans present.[36] Authority in moral matters in the Church is not seen by early or more recent Anglicans as concerned straightforwardly with the maintenance of standards of good behaviour; it is not simply a matter of ensuring that everyone who calls himself a Christian does 'good works'. If good works are the natural fruits of reconciliation with God, their absence, or acts which are not good, are indications that something is wrong in the soul. The Church's concern is with the infinitely complex problem of sin and not with a 'mere morality' of doing the right thing as an end in itself, or as a means to an end.

It is unsatisfactory to have to leave the question of good works in a hurry. It bulks far larger in the writings of the sixteenth century Anglican divines than the general question of the Church's authority in moral matters, and it remains a prime concern ecumenically to arrive at consensus here. In the recent Report of the Second Anglican-Roman Catholic International Commission, *Salvation and the Church*, we find, 'The works of the righteous performed in Christian freedom and in the love of God which the Holy Spirit gives are the object of God's commendation and receive his reward (Matthew 6.4; II Timothy 4.8; Hebrews 10.35, 11.6)'.)[37] The sixteenth century anxiety to balance the importance of right action *per se* against the necessary emphasis on human helplessness in the face of sin and man's utter dependence on grace and debt to the work of Christ, is as sharp as ever. But it tends to distract attention from one of the issues with which

---

35 Lambeth Occasional Reports, 1931-8 (London, 1948), p. 135.
36 *Ibid.*, p. 223.
37 (London, 1987), Paras. 19-24, here Para. 23.

we are immediately concerned in speaking of the Church's authority in moral matters: that is, whether there is an absolute standard of right and wrong which it is the Church's task to uphold, in all circumstances and in the same way everywhere; or whether it is appropriate for there to be autonomy in matters of morals in each ecclesial body.

The Lambeth Conference of 1920 took the view that 'The Christian Church has a code of morals as imperious in its claims as the rule of faith given in the Creeds' (Committee Report on problems of marriage and sexual morality). That of 1930 says that 'there are certain principles which must always be axiomatic for Christians' (Report on the Life and Witness of the Christian Community). This assertion of the existence of absolute moral rules is in tune with the position of the Roman Catholic community. 'The teacher and the model of all holiness is Christ ... Christ does not change in the course of centuries'.[38] Moral rules derive their finality from their divine source. The Thirty-Nine Articles speak of the Scriptures as containing everything necessary to salvation (6 and 20). The emphasis, for reasons of contemporary polemic, is upon what it is necessary to salvation to 'believe', rather than to 'do'; but it cannot be supposed that the framers of the Articles or their later interpreters would have wished to deny the Bible a divinely inspired authority on moral questions too.

Roman Catholic thinking has tended to the view that moral law is a natural law, 'implanted in rational creatures and inclining them to the right course of action and to their end', which 'is the eternal reason of God, the Creator and Ruler of the whole world'.[39] To this law, comprehended only by 'intellectual or rational natures', it is man's 'dignity' to respond in freedom and not under compulsion.[40] 'It is only as a free being that man can turn to what is good'.[41] But the crippling effects of sin upon the proper operation of the conscience of the individual is seen as making it necessary that the moral law should have teeth. 'The force of law consists in the imposing of obligations and the granting of rights'; 'it is ... founded on ... a true power to fix duties and define rights, as also to assign the necessary

---

38 Leo XIII, Letter, *Testem benevolentiae* to Cardinal Gibbons, Archbishop of Baltimore (1889). See Ombres, *op. cit.*

39 Leo XIII, Encyclical Letter, *Libertas Praestantissimum* (1888). Cf. *Proceedings* of the General Synod of the Church of England, 14 Feb. 1985, 'Anglicans have a special style of dealing with such matters' (the Bishop of Birmingham), p. 314.

40 *Ibid.*

41 Vatican II, 1965, *Gaudium et Spes*, 17. Cf. Leo XIII, *Libertas praestantissimum:* 'In man's free will ... or in the moral necessity for our voluntary acts to be in accordance with reason lies the very root of the necessity of law'; John XXIII, Encyclical Letter, *Pacem in Terris* (1963), cites Romans 2.15, 'The Creator of the world has imprinted in man's hesart an order which his conscience reveals to him and strongly enjoins him to obey'.

sanctions of reward and punishment for each and all of its commands'.[42]
These powers of fixing duties and defining rights have commonly been
thought of as operating in the Roman Catholic Church in a different mode
from that which, in protestantism, allows 'liberty' of individual conscience.
(A separate matter, it should be noted, from the question of 'public' and
'private' morality.) Yet the Lambeth Conference of 1948 thought it proper
to pass a series of Resolutions (39-49) on The Christian Way of Life; and if
such Resolutions have only 'moral authority' in the sense that they are not
coercive, nevertheless they can be seen as constituting an assertion of an
ecclesiastical authority in matters of morals.   The 1930 Report on the
Anglican Communion of the Lambeth Conference speaks of the necessity of
'a standard of conduct consistent with [a common] worship'. The Anglican
pattern has been to make the setting of moral standards by teaching and by
example the business of the Church, and in this there is no difference from
the longstanding practice of the Church of the West as a whole, or indeed
from the pattern of the universal Church through the ages.[43]

It is in tune with the setting of the moral rules for the individual within a
context of 'love of neighbour' that the Lambeth Conference of 1948 - in a
series of Resolutions on the doctrine of man and human rights (1-26) -
balanced 'rights' with 'duties' (Resolution 6). As an Encyclical Letter of
Pope John XXIII put it in 1963 (*Pacem in terris*), 'each particular right of
one man corresponds with a duty in the other persons, of acknowledging
and respecting that right'. There is thus both a relational and what we may
perhaps also call a 'relative' character to moral obligation within the
koinonia, which has to be balanced against the concept of an absolute moral
imperative. The notion of 'probable' opinion in moral matters has been
condemned by the Roman Catholic community (for example, decrees of
Alexander VII in 1665 and of Innocent XI in 1679). In 1956 an Instruction
of the Holy Office on 'situation ethics' ruled out the view that there can be
no 'objective right order determined by the law of nature and known with
certainty from that law' but only 'a certain intimate judgement and light of
the mind of each individual, by means of which, in the concrete situation in
which he is placed, he learns what he ought to do'. Nevertheless, it is
conceded that God 'permits evil to exist in the world' and that although
human law ... 'must not approve or will evil' it 'can allow it to exist "for
the sake of the common good"' (Leo XIII, Encyclical Letter, *Libertas
Praestantissimum*, 1888). The Lambeth Conference of 1930, in its Report
on the Life and Witness of the Christian Community, found it impossible to

---

[42] *Libertas Praestantissimum* (1888).

[43] On the notion that such matters are ultimately the business of the whole Church, see the
Bishop of St. Germans, *Proceedings* of the General Synod of the Church of England, 8
July, 1984, p. 510.

say 'Yet there exist moral situations which ...'. The question is whether we can legitimately proceed from the idea of a relational to that of a 'relative' treatment of the individual case in matters of morals by the Church, and whether it follows from the second possibility that each ecclesial body ought to act for itself. To suggest that the Church's task, as it emerges in the thinking of successive Lambeth Conferences, is to uphold standards conceived of as absolute, within a community whose human needs are of here and now, is the equivalent in the moral sphere of the concept of a faith which is always the same, and yet freshly expressed in every generation and very community. This balance of the absolute and unchanging, and the here and now, is expressed in the Committee Report of the 1920 Conference on problems of marriage and sexual morality as follows:

> The Clergy are commissioned to teach the Christian religion, which is to guide and hallow men's loves. To bear witness to the Divine Will, and to work for the fulfilment of that Will in the elevation and perfection of human life, is the very purpose of the Church's existence in the world.[44] If the Church is to leaven human society, it must faithfully uphold this standard at any cost, both by its teaching and by the exercise of discipline, refusing the privileges of the Church to those who transgress the divine commandment.

But 'it is greatly to be hoped', the Committee went on, 'that some standard work' on moral theology 'may be compiled by Anglican writers which will be accepted as embodying the Church's teaching in the light of *present-day* needs'.

This brings us to the question of the autonomy of particular Churches, local, diocesan, provincial or of different ages, to act independently in matters of morals.[45] The Lambeth Conference of 1920, in its Encyclical Letter, and its Resolutions called 'upon each Church of our Communion to develop its constitutional self-government'. The 1948 Committee Report on the Anglican Communion speaks of a 'series of provinces, each autonomous in its own sphere'. Resolution 52 of 1930 is more specific. 'Saving always the independence of the Divine Society, the Conference approves the association of Diocese or Provinces in the larger unity of a 'national Church' with or without the formal recognition of the Civil Government, as serving to give spiritual expression to the distinctive genius of races and

---

44 Cf. John XXII, Bull *Ad conditorem* to the Friars Minor (1322), 'The perfection of Christian life consists principally and essentially in charity'; Pius XI, Encyclical Letter *Quadragesimo anno* (1931) speaks of charity as the 'spiritual bond which unites' and as 'the main principle of stability in all institutions ... which aim at establishing social peace and promoting mutual help among men'.

45 See E. Dvornik's classic article, 'National Churches and the Church Universal, *Eastern Churches Quarterly* 5 (1943), pp. 172-218.

peoples'. Resolution 53 of the same Conference outlines the 'minimum organisation essential to provincial life' as a 'College of Synod of Bishops which will act corporately in dealing with questions concerning the faith, order and *discipline* of the Church'. The understanding here seems to be that such autonomous local Church-government has powers in moral matters. The Committee Report of the 1920 Lambeth Conference says as much. 'We admit of the right of a National Church to deal with ... cases' [concerning the breakdown of marriage] 'under such safeguards and disciplinary provisions as such Church may lay down'. This executive power in the moral sphere is envisaged by a Resolution of 1930 as being backed by an authority to give advice locally, if not legislate locally. Resolution 12 recommends that there should be established 'in the various branches of the Anglican Communion central councils which would study the problem of sex from the Christian standpoint and give advice to the responsible authorities in diocese or parish or theological college as to methods of approach and lines of instruction'.

It would seem that the Lambeth Conferences at least have not as yet directly and systematically addressed a series of key questions here: where provincial autonomy ends in decision-making on matters of faith, order and morals; where the establishment of moral rules ends and 'discipline' begins; what is the sphere of provincial or diocesan jurisdiction in matters of discipline in relation to that of the minister with pastoral charge or 'cure of souls' locally within a particular congregation; mercy; whether it can really be the case that Anglicans claim no more than a 'moral authority', that is, a non-coercive authority, an authority of example, working by loyalty to the fellowship, when at least in the sphere of authority in matters of morals there is and always has been provision for punitive sanctions, both legal and excommunicative. Above all, it seems likely to be of considerable ecumenical value for Anglicans to begin to work out where their tradition places them in relation to the ancient penitential system in the light of all this. It is in that area that the question of authority in matters of faith was most fully and painstakingly worked out in the centuries before the Reformation, and it has been a hindrance to protestant thinking on these matters since that both 'works' and 'penance' have become terms hard to use outside the context of polemic. The late-mediaeval abuses of the penitential system have tended to blot out for protestants that which was profoundly merciful and practical in it.

Chapter Ten

Towards a common faith and order

It has always been acceptable among Christians that there should be variation of opinion on certain matters of faith and local variation in liturgical practice. (Predestination, for example, is not an article of faith to all; Article 20 of the Anglican Thirty-Nine Articles says that the Church has 'power to decree rites and ceremonies'.) On the other hand, some matters of faith and order have consistently been deemed so fundamental that those differing in belief (the Arians, for example) have been regarded as heretics, and those in breach of order (such as the Donatists), schismatics.

A good deal of Christian scholarly effort, especially since the later Middle Ages, has gone into the attempt to define the difference between matters which exclude from communion or divide Churches; and matters of relative indifference. John of Ragusa at the Council of Basle in 1433 spoke of Scripture as containing all things necessary to salvation (cf. Article 6 of the Thirty-Nine Articles);[1] seventeenth and eighteenth century authors juggled with 'fundamentals', 'essentials', 'elementaries', as well as with the concept of that which is 'necessary to salvation'. There was discussion of the nature and content of the *depositum;* this last raised again by the Chicago bishops in their Quadrilateral of 1886. The Lambeth Quadrilateral of 1888[2] which grew out of it proposed a minimal four points as notes or marks of the true Church: Scripture, Creeds, Sacraments and the 'historic episcopate': 'locally adapted', but nevertheless constituting a fundamental of order.

Over against these attempts to list unchanging basics, other thinkers set a variety of what might be called 'dynamic' accounts. In the Middle Ages there is talk of implicit and explicit in Scripture, of an unwrapping of revelation; images of stream and source; of the growth of a seed; of progress and development in what looks very like a 'Whig theory' of the development of doctrine, implicitly or explicitly challenged in post-Reformation centuries; the contention that the Church was most truly herself in the apostolic age. The most recent model has been one of 'pluriformity', the acceptance of the inevitability, the rightness, even the

---

[1] On John of Ragusa, see my *The Logic and Language of the Bible: the Road to Reformation* (Cambridge, 1985), pp. 39-41 and 118.

[2] See *Quadrilateral at One Hundred*, ed. J. Robert Wright, (Ohio, London and Oxford, 1988).

desirability of variety of opinion and diversity of order, within certain limits.[3] To this school of thought belong the theme of 'inculturation', the doctrine of Anglican provincial autonomy, strongly developed for practical reasons since 1867,[4] Vatican II's acceptance of the ecclesial being of other Churches.

In all this the discussion of fundamentals of faith has tended to outstrip that of questions of essential order, and relatively little attention has been given to the relationship of the two as both 'fundamental'. It is becoming ecumenically urgent to think the matter through. The thrust of ecumenical conversations during the last two decades has been primarily to try to reach agreement on matters of faith and on the theology of order. It is becoming impossible to speak of 'the truths we share' as a basis[5] for moving towards a unity of order. The prerequisite is a common understanding of the nature and form of essentials or fundamentals of order, and their interdependence with shared truths of faith.

When John Henry Newman published his *Development of Christian Doctrine* he had just become a Roman Catholic; the book was in the press when he made his decision.[6] He addressed his argument to the question 'Which is the true Church?'[7] In his day he could have seen no alternative to

3 See Rowan Williams, 'The unity of Christian Truth', *New Blackfriars*, Special Issue, February, 1989, p. 85.
4 See my article 'Anglican Conciliar Theory: Provincial Autonomy and the Present Crisis' in *One in Christ* (1989), 34-52.
5 *The Niagara Report*, Anglican-Lutheran Consultation on Episcope, 1987, Paragraphs 60-80.
6 Newman, *Letters and Diaries*, ed. C.S. Dessain (Oxford, 1961), IX.25-6 and following, gives the correspondence between Newman and Bishops Wiseman, over whether the book would be acceptable to Roman Catholic authorities. See in particular the letters of 7 Nov., 9 Nov., 18 Nov., 1845.
7 Newman put his difficulty in a few words in the Advertisement to the First Edition of *Development*. In the *Tracts for the Times*, eleven years earlier, he had already acknowledged 'the high gifts, and the strong claims of the Church of Rome' but he had seen an 'obstacle' to 'rushing into communion with her'. 'The following Work is directed', he says, 'towards its removal'. The obstacle was the belief that the true faith was not to be found at Rome. Once he became convinced that it was, he could no longer remain an Anglican.
   Newman was not to be the last Vicar of the University Church of St. Mary in Oxford to feel bound in conscience to become a Roman Catholic. But the circumstances of the mid-nineteenth century in which that appeared to him the only possible course of action have changed, and with them the way in which the questions about the development of doctrine can most usefully be framed. In Newman's book and in the writings bearing on the topic which immediately preceded it (especially the University Sermons), the focus is upon the nature of the 'proofs' which can be trusted ('evidences', 'probabilities'), upon old debates over 'natural and revealed' religion (the classic work here is William Paley's *View of the Evidences of Christianity* (1794), with his *Natural Theology* (1802).), in short upon the grounds on which the individual may give his assent to truths of faith.

the individual's acting in conscience to 'join' that Church which he had come to believe was indeed the true Church. In our own time it is possible to look at a future united Church, and to seek to bring the Churches together as a whole. The task is not to identify, as Newman sought to do, the *locus* of a decision-making authority in one Church, but to enable all the Churches to come to agreement together on matters of faith and order. We can take a larger view of the providential plan for the 'development' of doctrine than Newman and his contemporaries were able to do. The lessons of the disasters of the Church's history, when it has been divided by mutual hostility, must be taken up into the common understanding of the faith. Within that larger frame of reference, it clearly cannot be possible to speak of a 'perfected', that is to say, completed doctrinal development,[8] for we have not yet reached a point where all Christians can affirm a common faith in a manner which mends divisions.[9] Nor can we come yet to a common order. At this stage we are trying to describe a complex constant which is, paradoxically, both final and yet capable of re-expression in every age. We are learning to think, not in terms of the 'standards' and 'bindingness' of the nineteenth century, but of authoritative pronouncements which are also interim statements.

That is, in any case, a historically more accurate description, and provided it is understood that these are attempts to put into words for a given time and place what remains a permanent truth, nothing is put at risk. In matters of order, as in matters of faith, the important thing is to err on the safe side.[10] In the life of the Church disputes about order have to be settled without taking risks with the validity of the sacraments. The problem before us is how to recognise the seal of authority on ecumenical statements of common faith and bring to a future united Church that common order which is much harder than common faith to restore. The question goes beyond the point at which individual Churches can declare their respective acceptances through their own decision-making machinery, to the stage when they can, as it were, affix a common seal.

Newman enlarged these by entering a plea for moral certainty and the action of conscience. (See Owen Chadwick, *From Bossuet to Newman* (Cambridge, 1957).) He set in parallel with them a case for the development of doctrine which is to be measured by a series of tests, and which is seen as working in part by means of a collective exercise of conscience in the community.

8   Cf. K. Rahner, *Theological Investigations*, I (1961, p. 41, 'The perfected law of doctrinal development may only be laid down when the whole, unique process has reached its term'.

9   This is the thrust of the Niagara Report's recommendations, for example.

10   Daniel Waterland, *On Fundamentals*, p. 85, 'in case of just and reasonable doubt ... the known rule, is to choose the *safer* side'.

Personal and ecclesial essentials

Two strains commonly appear in the system. Henry Hammond (1605-60) drew a distinction in his essay on *Fundamentals*, between the necessary elements in a Creed which was to be used for the 'disciplining of all nations' and which was thus 'necessary to the discharge of the apostolical office, which was to reap whole fields, to bring in whole cities and nations to Christ'; and what it is 'absolutely necessary in every single convert' to hear and believe (*Fundamentals*, pp. 78-9).[11]   He distinguishes in this way between what is 'necessary to salvation' and has personal and individual reference; and what is necessary to the being and mission of the Church, that is, to the 'discharge of the apostolical office'. Daniel Waterland (1683-1740) preferred to equate the 'essentials of the Christian fabric or system' with 'fundamentals considered in a *relative* view to particular persons, in which respect they are frequently called *necessaries*, as being ordinarily necessary to salvation'. They 'coincide', he thinks, 'and are indeed the same thing' (p. 77).   Nevertheless, he accepts the view that the 'terms of communion' are stricter than 'the necessary terms of salvation'. That is to say, the Church excludes from communion many whom it regards as erring fundamentally', but it 'dare not condemn' them 'absolutely to everlasting perdition' (p. 78).[12]   Both are aware, although they seek to resolve it in different ways, of a tension between what is fundamental in the sense that without it no-one can be saved, and what is fundamental in the sense of being of the *esse* of the Church.

Primitive or developed doctrine

A second constant tension is observed by many authors. On the one hand there is a strong consensus in favour of the view that the fundamentals are to be found only in Scripture and the practice of the primitive community. The Church has authority to teach 'that only which she received, being delivered unto her from the Lord by the doctrine of the prophets and apostles', as Bullinger puts it (1504-75).[13] Hammond extends 'those first and purest ages' to three hundred years, but he, too, deems the primitive to

---

11 Henry Hammond, *On Fundamentals*.
12 But compare Waterland, p. 91, 'Another ... rule is, that whatever Scripture has expressly declared necessary, or commanded us to believe under pain of damnation, or of exclusion from Christian communion, that is fundamental, and nothing else is'; note, too, Waterland's distinction between 'elementaries', 'fundamentals' and 'essentials'.
13 Bullinger, Fifth *Decade*, Sermon 1, ed. T. Harding, Parker Society (Cambridge, 1852), pp. 44 ff.

be fundamental.[14] 'Every doctrine must be deemed true', he says, 'which conspires with the apostolical Churches, which are the wombs and originals whence the faith came out'.[15] Waterland refers to those who 'take Scripture truths and fundamental truths to be tantamount and reciprocal', although he would not go so far himself.[16] It was Newman's opinion that the primitive and fundamental had a cogency, though one in danger of being 'weakened by lapse of time', so that as the Church fell into the danger of losing touch with the Apostolic Tradition 'the imposition of doctrinal tests ... became necessary'.[17] He himself had a profound sense of being brought back into contact with the beginnings when he became a Roman Catholic. He was able to take down from his shelves the volumes of Athanasius or Basil and no longer feel himself 'an outcast'. 'I kissed them with delight', he says.[18] John Wordsworth, lecturing in Aberdeen in 1902 put it squarely. 'By "fundamentals", I personally understand those truths and institutions which we can trace back to the first age of the Church, and on which all its after life is based'. 'Why', he asks, 'do we attach so much importance to primitive times? It is not merely because they come first, and therefore necessarily colour all that comes after, but because there was undoubtedly a more general outpouring of the Holy Spirit and a closer brotherhood of believers in the first 200 years of Christian history than in any other age'. He makes the point that this seems 'a much safer enumeration than that of Waterland and others like him ... who start from some central idea, such as that of the Christian covenant, and consider what truths or institutions are necessary to support it'.[19]

This view, which has its mediaeval antecedents in movements which pursued the ideal of the *vita apostolica*,[20] is not without capacity for life and growth, but it takes as its foundation the notion of essentials laid down once and for all at the beginning, a *depositum*. Hammond, for example, sees the

---

14 Hammond, *On Schism*, vòl. *cit.*, VIII.7.
15 Hammond, in *Of Heresy*, vol. *cit.*, pp. 333-4, on Vincent of Lérins, 'For the universality of time, that must be cautiously understood; not so as to signify is a prejudice to any doctrine, if in some one or more ages it have not been universally received; for then there could be no hereticks at any time in the world: but so as to extend to the first and purest, and not only to the later ages of the Church'.
16 Waterland, p. 88.
17 Newman, *The Arians of the Fourth Century* (1833), Fourth ed. (London, 1876), II.1, p. 133.
18 Newman, *Certain Difficulties Felt by Anglicans in Catholic Teaching* (1864 and 1874), (London, 1876), p. 3.
19 John Wordsworth, *The Bearing of the Study of Church History on some problems of Home Reunion*, Murtle Lecture, Aberdeen, 23 Feb., 1902 (London, 1902), pp. 10-12).
20 This was the Franciscan ideal, and that of many twelfth century reformers and innovators in the religious life.

Apostolic foundation as the *depositum* given to each Church (p. 77), and the
Chicago Quadrilateral of 1886 speaks equally readily of 'the substantial
deposit of Christian Faith and Order committed by Christ and his Apostles
to the Church unto the end of the world'. Alongside talk of the *depositum* it
is possible to find the suggestion that the basics are first principles of the
sort envisaged by Aristotle in the *Posterior Analytics*, that is, 'that wherein
the very essence or subsistence of the subject is contained'.[21] Waterland, for
example, quoting Sherlock, suggests that they are 'necessary to the very
being of Christianity like the first principles of any art or science'.[22] That is
to suggest that they are both 'given', and essential, or 'of the essence'.

In tension with this picture of things which made the primitive
fundamental, were certain aspects of the doctrine of 'development' as it was
explored in the nineteenth century. For Newman there was no serious
difficulty here. He believed that what had been formulated as doctrine in
the course of the Church's history, and had received her seal of authority,
was not new, but always a statement in full, of principles implicit, or
existing in miniature, in the primitive community's understanding of the
faith. He tried to trace hints that this was so in his book on *Development*.
His friend and critic Mozley thought him wrong to believe that the the
Church's teachings could be regarded with confidence as no more than
unravellings of truths always understood in principle. In order to
demonstrate this, he reviewed the possible understandings of what is
involved in 'development'. He himself did not see great force in the analogy
of organic growth (as from a seed) for, as he pointed, out, it 'makes the
question of truth a question of quantity; and the biggest development,
whatever it be, the truest'.[23] And the idea that 'all grows out of one seed' ...
'gets over the ground of later doctrines with bold assurance; but when it
comes to the fundamental ones, it stops and wavers'.[24] That is to say, as
William Palmer pointed out, it throws it seriously open to question whether
doctrine as understood and formulated in the early Church is not in some
way inferior. It suggests that 'all appeal to the ancient Christian writers, the
customs of the early Church, nay, to Scripture itself ... is absurd', and 'that
the most recent deductions of reason in reference to religious truth, as
representing the most advanced state of intellectual progress, are of the
highest authority'.[25] That had been seriously put forward as a hypothesis by

21 Waterland, p. 74.
22 Waterland, p. 79, quoting Sherlock, *Vindication of the Defence of Stillingfleet*, p. 256.
23 J.B. Mozley, Review of Newman's *Development, The Christian Remembrancer*, xiii
    (1847), 117-265, p. 128. Cf. *Development* I.ii.2.3-4.
24 *Ibid.*, pp. 261, 264 and 216, and *From Bossuet to Newman*, pp. 25, 93-4 and 98.
25 *From Bossuet to Newman*, p. 92.

William Law and in Germany,[26] and was liked by those Deists of the previous century who had thought it would have been unjust in God to vouchsafe a special and necessary revelation only at a late stage in history.[27] Newman was certainly not unaware that a raw theory of progress and advancement in the development of doctrine had such drawbacks; he went to a good deal of trouble to underline the importance of the constant checks and balances which made development an unfolding of a single constant principle and neither addition nor change. Nevertheless, he could also say that 'Scripture ... begins a series of developments which it does not finish' (University Sermon, XIII, p. 335).[28]

It is the second of our two tensions which has received most attention in theological discussion in almost every century, and before we come to the first, we need to look briefly at some of the options which have been canvassed for resolving the dilemma that it can neither be satisfactory to say that doctrine has so 'developed' that earlier generations of Christians did not possess the faith in its fulness; nor conversely to characterise that which it was possible to say in the apostolic age as uniquely a better or higher or fuller Christian truth. That would mean, as Robert Rainy pointed out during the controversy occasioned by Newman's book, that it would be necessary to say of any doctrinal formulation of later centuries, 'It makes its appearance too late. If it had been authorised, it would have been heard of before. If it were part of the faith once delivered to the saints, it would not have been so late in putting in an appearance to claim its right'.[29] Rainy himself thought it important to underline the ecclesial task here, 'to assert and vindicate development of doctrine as a function of the Church of Christ, belonging to her duty, connected with the right use of her privileges, and indeed indispensable to her life'.[30] The role of the Church is, in other words, central to the question whether the fundamentals are simply the matters of faith and order clearly discernible in the early Church as it brought the canon of Scripture into being, or continue to rest in the hands of the living Church.

The tension between the 'primitive' and the 'developed' theories of doctrine was most commonly addressed by means of images and analogies

---

26 William Law, *An Appeal to all who doubt the Truths of the Gospel* (London, 1740), p. 85 and J.A.L. Wegscheider, *Institutiones Theologiae Christianae Dogmaticae* (1813), cf. Toon, p. 29.

27 *From Bossuet to Newman,* p. 85.

28 Newman, *University Sermons*, are ed. D.M. MacKinnon and J.D. Holmes (London, 1970).

29 R. Rainy, *Delivery and Development of Christian Doctrine* (Edinburgh, 1874), p. 7, delivered as the Cunningham Lectures, Edinburgh, 1873.

30 Rainy, pp. 183-5.

designed to make it clear how the Church in history had proceeded from basics to its present formulations. In that way the relationship of doctrine today to apostolic doctrine could, it was hoped, be clarified; and correspondingly for order. As Hammond put it, the foundation was 'laid by the Apostles and other such master builders', on which the Church was to be built, 'so to the superstructing Christian obedience among men' (p. 73). The superstructure could be seen as meeting a practical need for moral guidance and a missionary need, 'to the peopling or replenishing, or bringing in proselyted to the Church' (*ibid.*), rather than as adding to the faith given once and for all. An alternative device was to see the whole of Christian doctrine as a single article with its implications drawn out. For Luther that single article was faith in Christ and his all-sufficient saving work. For Daniel Waterland it was the notion of a covenant. From this he infers that there must be a Founder and principal Covenanter, a subject with whom the covenant can be made, a charter of foundation, a Mediator, conditions to be performed, aids or means to make their performance possible, and sanctions to bind the covenant (p. 80).[31] In his view, this scheme 'amounts to the same' as using the 'general and comprehensive article of Salvation by Christ' (p. 87).

Fundamentals and the history of truths

Not all the truths which can thus be drawn out of, or built up upon, a foundation principle are of equal weight. The notion of a hierarchy of truths was well developed in the seventeenth and eighteenth centuries.[32] It is, nevertheless, important that the lesser truths are 'joined with, or resolve into' greater ones which are 'valuable for their own intrinsic weight and worth', and which touch on 'the main substance of the Christian faith, worship, morality' (Waterland, p. 89). They are not, in other words, to be set aside as unimportant. Indeed, 'those inferior points may by accident become fundamental, if the denying them, in some certain circumstances, should inevitably carry with it a denial of the Divine authority of sacred Writ' (*Ibid.*, pp. 89-90). Waterland is opposed to the reductionism canvassed, for example, by Grotius in his *Meletius*.

In his unpublished *Meletius*, or *Letter on those things which are agreed among Christians* (c. 1609-11), Grotius puts forward several practical rules for ecumenists.[33] He draws a comparison between precepts, or rules for

---

31 Rowan Williams, *op. cit.*

32 Waterland, p. 74, lists Hoornbeech, Velthysius, Spanheim and Turretin as basing on Scripture the view that there is a distinction between 'weightier matters and the matters less weighty'.

33 Edited by G.H.M. Posthumus Meyjes (Leiden, 1988).

right living; and *decreta*, by which he means the whole conspectus of *fides quae*. When Christians quarrel, he says, it is usually about doctrine not ethics. He puts that down to human nature. Seneca was right to say that people would rather argue than get on with their lives.[34] It is harder work to struggle with oneself than to engage in a war of words with other people (89, p. 101). And when there is a dispute over a point of right practice, it is usually not divisive. Irenaeus pointed out to Victor, Bishop of Rome, that although practice varies over how many days of fasting are appropriate before Easter, *nihilominus concordia retinetur*, that is not a Church-dividing issue (90, pp. 101-2). Such differences are recognised not to concern fundamentals of ethics, but to belong to the category of those matters which everyone decides so as to preserve order (*ordinis servandi causa*), and where there is freedom of conscience (90, p. 101).

Disputes about doctrine have different characteristics. Many of them concern words; if certain terms are avoided, *consensus apparet* (90, p. 102). Others arise because something which is not fundamental is being treated as though it were essential to salvation (*ibid.*). The first mistake to put right here is the tendency to frame more dogmas than are necessary. It cannot be possible for everyone to agree about everything, and once a point of doctrine has been stated and claimed by a party, it is very difficult for them to yield, for their pride in their *secta* has become bound up with it (90, p. 102).

Grotius sees the remedy for this as lying in two things. The list of articles deemed necessary to salvation to believe should be kept to a minimum, and those the most obvious (*maxima evidentia*). And we should recognise that for our opponents we are heretics just as they seem heretics to us. They believe they have the truth, just as we do. Sincerity of belief out of love for God ought to be respected. We should not indulge in polemic and recrimination but explain our position to them in a friendly way (91, p. 102).

Grotius showed the manuscript of the Meletius to four of his friends, and the views of three of them survive in letters.[35] With Antonius Walaeus there was a continuing exchange, three letters from Walaeus and two from Grotius. Walaeus queried Grotius' contention that it is best to keep to a minimum the number of points on which it is deemed essential for Christians to agree (p. 169, referring to *Meletius* 3, pp. 76 and 91, 102). Walaeus was a Calvinist, and he feared that some of the points of difference in doctrine which Grotius was prepared to dismiss as non-essential were by no means unimportant. 'Many dogmas held by the Papists completely

---

[34] Cf. Seneca, *Letters* 95.13 and 108.23.
[35] Meyjes, Introduction, p. 44 ff.

overturn the faith', he says (pp. 169-70). He would also like to have seen an exhortation to read Scripture more strongly pressed (p. 170). In reply, Grotius accepts the criticism, but points to a further difficulty about the Roman Catholic hierarchy of truths. François Dujon (a professor at Leiden) used to jest that Roman Catholic 'error in fundamentals was forgivable as long as they did not depart from what was fundamental': *ita in fundamentis errare, ut a fundamentis non aberrarent*, and Grotius agrees (p. 171).[36] This wry paradox summed up the difficulty in which contemporary protestants thought they found themselves.

Grotius believes that those things which are the most dangerous beliefs of Roman Catholics (*periculosissima*) can be interpreted according to the principles he has put forward. There must be an authority to which all must bow, and accept if it proves their views false. The teachings of the Roman Catholic Church, and the private opinions of the individual, are subject alike to the measure of that which all Christians have always held (p. 171). This is *consensus* (*Meletius*, 6, p. 77). Walaeus was not so sanguine. He replied to Grotius' letter to say that it seemed to him that while it was certainly true that Roman Catholic teaching included the fundamentals of faith at times, nevertheless, they 'build up with one hand what they throw down with the other' (p. 174). Those who build in rotten wood are not really building on the foundation as they should (p. 174 and cf. I Corinthians 3.12). They add to the fundamentals things which take away their true meaning (*veri fundamenti vim omnino tollunt*). There can, for example, be no consistency between their perfectly correct assertion that Christ is the propitiator for our sins and their teaching that the merits of monks, confessors and martyrs can be dispensed by pontifical authority in the form of indulgences (p. 174). So Christ is made useless (*inutilis*) to them, not because they deny him, but because they try to add to his work 'righteousness by keeping the law' (p. 174). They urge Christians to call on God through Christ their intercessor; but at the same time they teach people to put their trust in the invocation of the saints and the cult of images. It is as though they gave people good food and also poison (*ibid.*). Building on the foundation in materials which will not perish in the fire is the way to salvation (*ibid.*).

Walaeus was not convinced by Grotius' argument that the points peculiar to Roman Catholic teaching could be shown by his principles to be errors, leaving a large part of their faith in common with that of other Christians (p. 174). He was not prepared to regard such 'errors' as comparatively trivial, or to take the view that sickness in one part of a body does not make the whole body sick (pp. 174-5).

---

[36] Junius (François Dujon) discusses the point in *De Ecclesia, Opera Theologica*, II.997-1023.

'I agree with you', replied Grotius, 'that there is in the Roman Church something in common with other Churches, and something which is peculiar to that Church'. The one is Christian, the other for the most part antichristian. But he argues that not all matters of faith are of the same *auctoritas*. Those which are matters of consensus among all Christians (*communia*) must be held with a particular *notitia* which is not required for the others. The first are necessary for salvation, and must be taught as beyond question. The others are *non necessaria*. However, Grotius recognises that there are grave matters at issue between Christians, 'and especially between us and the papists', which are difficult to resolve. But that ought not to lead us to behave as though there were no common ground between us, or as though we shared nothing but the name of Christian (p. 177).

Another friend, Petrus Cunaeus, commented that had he been writing about the things Christians have in common he would have proposed many fewer points, and treated them rather differently (p. 180).

There seem to have been several reasons why Grotius did not publish the *Meletius*. It was not a propitious moment for calling for peace.[37] He felt he could not revise either his central hypothesis or his section on grace and free will, as Walaeus had suggested he should.[38] And in time he wrote the *De Veritate* which perhaps made the *Meletius* appear redundant.

Grotius raises a number of points of modern ecumenical relevance in this aborted treatise. He argues that the attempt to state a common faith together should not be ambitious to include everything, but should make a distinction between what is essential and what can be left to conscience. The endeavour should be to keep essentials to a minimum. He identifies consensus as the highest authority in decision-making in matters of faith. He recognises that consensus can be possible only on a relatively small number of essentials, not only because that is human nature, but because that is also the lesson of history and the pattern of tradition. The issue of substance on which Walaeus disagreed with him was whether such an approach is adequate as a means of achieving unity among Christians. He took the case of the differences between Roman Catholics and protestants as his example, and argued that one could not, as it were, single out the good parts of a Church's teaching and disregard the rest. The system needed to be considered as a whole, so that the relationship of the essentials to the rest was clearly understood, and it was apparent whether the points identified as fundamentals were not only common, but also agreed by all parties to be fundamental.

---

[37] Meyjes, p. 59.
[38] *Ibid.*, p. 57.

Waterland agrees that it is not enough to take as fundamental what everyone, even Jews and Moslems, can agree upon; it is not enough to take a single article of faith by itself; there must be a sense of the interconnectedness of Christian truths, of their interdependency; above all, of the need for something more to keep a man a Christian than it takes to make him one (Waterland, pp. 97 - 100). It is in such reflections that we seen the discussions about fundamentals of faith abutting onto the area of order, as Waterland explores the place of the good life and of the Church's role.

This difficult area of the relationship between matters fundamental in faith and matters fundamental in order had been perceived generations earlier by Francis Bacon, in his *Advancement of Learning*. He suggests that fundamentals of faith are non-negotiable. It is of these that Christ said, 'He that is not with us is against us' (Matthew 12.30). In other matters there may be pluriformity. 'He that is not against us, is with us' (Luke 9.50). 'So we see the coat of our Saviour was entire without seam; and so is the doctrine of the Scripture in itself; but the garment of the Church was of divers colours, and yet not divided'.[39] It is on this basis that an attempt must be made 'to define what, and of what latitude those points are, which do make men merely aliens and disincorporate from the Church of God' (p. 214). He does not note the paradox that such matters of indifference as to unity in order are also, on his own statement, 'perfective, being matter of further building and perfection upon one and the same foundation'.[40] Hammond suggests an answer to this difficulty. It is possible to see, in the variety of understanding of the one truth, and in many ecclesial bodies, a means of 'each supplying the defects and infirmities of others' (*On Schism*, I.3, p. 196). Thus the non-fundamentals are able to be 'perfective', in Bacon's sense without being 'required', so as to become themselves fundamental to Christian unity. Bacon himself concedes that it is unrealistic to expect 'completeness' in 'divinity'.[41]

The historical dimension

Newman's hypothesis that 'the discovery of new truths' is no more than the gaining of 'further insight into the primitive and received sense of Scripture passages, ... by meditating upon them, and bringing out their one idea more completely' (University Sermons, p. 89) implies, as we have seen, that

---

39 Francis Bacon, *The Advancement of Learning*, XXV.9, ed. G.W. Kitchin (London, 1973), pp. 213-4.
40 *Ibid.*, XXV.8, p. 213.
41 *Ibid.*, XX V.8, p. 215.

developments form a single and uniform body'.[42]   Writing in his autobiography about the position of his mind since 1845, he reflected, 'Nothing ... can be presented to me, in time to come, as part of the faith, but what I ought already to have received, and hitherto have been kept from receiving, (if so) merely because it has not been brought home to me' (Apo, p. 253).   Moberly perceived an anomaly here, between this *a priori* philosophical theory' and the kinds of claims it obliges us to make for history. He asks, 'Are the theologians of the primitive and mediaeval times, the very theologians of the times of Luther and the Council of Trent, themselves to be understood to have held implicit theories to defend implicit doctrines? Are they to be thought to have believed what they did not state, on grounds which they did not urge?'[43] 'The pressure of philosophy' is seen as pushing Newman's historical judgement out of shape. Moberly shrewdly puts his finger on a real difficulty of historical method here, for Newman certainly refers his tests of development to history, trying them out against events for proof. But the development of doctrine is not straightforwardly measurable against history, as Newman also saw, and history cannot in itself tell us what is new and therefore heretical; or an unfolding of an existing idea, and therefore not.[44]

Identifying the basics: faith and order

A number of attempts were made to list 'fundamentals' or 'essentials'. Bacon divides them into those concerned with faith; those which have to do with manners (natural, moral and positive law); the liturgical essentials ('the reciprocal acts between God and man; which, on the part of God, are the preaching of the Word, and the sacraments, which are seals to the covenant, or as the visible Word; and on the part of man, invocation of the name of God and ... prayers or confessions'; principles of government in the Church) (XXV.20-2, p. 219 f.). For Hammond, they are 'Jesus Christ as the one only foundation'; him crucified, raised, manifest; baptism, the creeds and instruction in the faith, confirmation, the Eucharist, with preaching, pastoral care and discipline in the Church (*Fundamentals*, Chapters 2-19). For the Chicago Convention of 1886, too, the fundamentals are the deposit not only of faith but also of order. Undeveloped though the implications are, it is almost universally seen that fundamentals of order go along with fundamentals of faith.

---

[42] G. Moberly, *The Sayings of the Great Forty Days, with an examination of Newman's Theory of Development* (fourth ed., London, 1871), p. xvii.

[43] *Ibid.*, p. xxi.

[44] *From Bossuet to Newman*, pp. 88, 120, 153-4.

Human and divine

The underlying difficulty in all this had been clearly (and frequently) stated
by the sixteenth century reformers. It brings us back to the first tension,
between personal and ecclesial essentials and fundamentals. At issue here is
the problem of determining what is human (and therefore subject to error),
and what is of divine origin (and therefore secure). Newman took up the
point in his University Sermon on 'Implicit and Explicit Reason' in 1840.
'Inspiration is defective', he argues, 'not in itself, but in consequence of the
medium it uses and the beings it addresses ... neither can man compass, nor
can his hundred tongues utter, the mysteries of the spiritual world, and
God's appointments in this. This vast and intricate scheme of things cannot
... be represented through or to the mind of man; and inspiration, in
undertaking to do so, necessarily lowers what is divine to raise what is
human.[45] It was, for many, open to question whether 'Christ's Church has
... been left to discover or gather His truth by ... collation or inference',
whether, in short, there is a place for the formulation of doctrines at all.

R.D. Hampden, in his Bampton Lecture of 1832 (published 1833) on *The
Scholastic Philosophy considered in its relation to Christian Theology*, took
as his subject 'the importance of human means concerned in the
establishment and maintenance of the Gospel truth' (Preface, p. vii).
Hampden was not the first to propose the question in more or less this form.
William Law, a century earlier, had asked whether it is presumptuous to
think that human reason has a place among theological authorities and tried
to distinguish between the 'delivery' of a doctrine and the human 'measure'
by which it must be received.[46] But Hampden sparked a controversy. He
insisted that theological dogmas are merely 'human authorities'. Scripture
contains, he says, 'no doctrines. What we read there is matter of fact'. 'The
facts of Scripture remain the same through all ages - not so the theories
raised upon them'.[47] William Palmer, one of the Tractarians, canvassed the
view that Christian truth is dependent not upon 'external evidences', but 'on
the movements of the human mind'.[48] His response shows that all this was
in origin a contribution to the 'evidences' debate, but Hampden seemed to

[45] p. 268.

[46] William Law, *The Case of Reason or Natural Religion (1731)*, Works, II (1892), and cf.
Bossuet to Newman, p. 97.

[47] R.D. Hampden, *The Scholastic Philosophy Considered in its Relation to Christian
Theology*, Bampton Lectures of 1832, published Oxford, 1833), p. 374, and see H.
Christmas, *A Concise History of the Hampden Controversy* (London, 1848), pp. 149-
50).

[48] William Palmer, *The Doctrine of Development and of Conscience*, p. 88.

his adversaries to be going beyond the familiar territory of 'natural and revealed religion'. His liberalism was anathema to both Evangelicals and Tractarians, but for different reasons. The Tractarians and those of like mind could not allow that there was no divine gift to the Church which made it possible for it to speak authoritatively. Evangelicals like Robert Rainy wanted to ask how far we could take it that the Bible was designed to be used for the purpose of 'laying down doctrines'[49] and what the role of human effort might be in so using it. He sides with Hampden so far as to say that 'as uttered by the believer and the Church, doctrine is formally human'; but he insists that 'it is the human confession of the divine gift', 'truth as it has been proposed in forms of human thought and feeling, clothed in human words, dwelling in the minds of human messengers, and bodied forth from their lips and pen'.[50]

We see here the tensions of a long-standing disagreement over the 'human' face of doctrine. On one side stand those who say that, though human in formulation, it is to be trusted because it speaks with the voice of the Church through the ages. On the other, those who reply that, though human in formulation, it is to be trusted insofar as it may be regarded as incarnating Scripture. In the midst stand the new 'liberals', who thought that because it was human, it could not have the status of fact at all.

The Victorian William Palmer detected something of the anxiety on all sides to save what is precious and essential here. He comments that those 'sectarians' who 'have denied the validity of deductions or inferences from Scripture, or the certainty of any interpretations of it', and who say we must use the 'express words of Scripture for Christian doctrines or Church discipline' are presenting an 'exaggeration and perversion' of what is nevertheless a 'truth ... of the highest importance'. They were trying desperately hard to save the principle that 'Divine revelation is one and immutable'.[51] They did not want to see Scripture's sovereignty denied. In each case, the view taken of the human role in the formulation of doctrine depends upon the nature of the threat that is perceived. Opposing Dr. Hampden, W.J. Irons of Brompton in Middlesex, framed fifty-two propositions. Among them is one which suggests that 'the secret motive of the Christian clergy from age to age has been the obtaining of power over their fellow Christians; and that to succeed in this, they have moulded the whole system of Christianity afresh'.[52] Irons' heavy irony about anticlericalism is a mockery of the opinion put forward in all seriousness by

---

[49] Toon, *op. cit.*, pp. 38-9.
[50] *Ibid.*
[51] Palmer, *op. cit.*, p. 89.
[52] W.J. Irons, *Fifty-Two Propositions: A Letter to the Rev. Dr. Hampden* (London, 1848), Proposition 2.

many sixteenth century - and earlier - reformers which informed much anti-Christian polemic. Another of Irons' mocking propositions is designed to defend the very doctrinal basis of the Church of England: 'That the Articles and Creeds of the Church of England are founded on a false philosophy, and it is devoutly to be wished, that, as they cannot be defended, they may eventually be got rid of'.[53] Here again the Church itself is seen to be at risk if no human role is allowed.

Hampden's central thesis, that the history of scholasticism demonstrates that human reasoning is more likely than not to lead to chaos and controversy, was also contested by Irons, on much the same grounds as John Hey had used in his *Lectures in Divinity* (Cambridge, 1796). Hey thought that a controversy could even be beneficial, and that incidental good could come out of it, because it was one of the appointed means by which human minds can be stimulated to stretch themselves to the limit in the study of divine perfection.[54] The 'human' element in the making of doctrine was being reviewed along lines identifiable with those of earlier controversy, in which what was ultimately at stake was the question of the authority of the human community in the Church to make doctrine.

We need to look at a series of aspects of the working of this 'human element'. First comes the assent of the individual, to which Newman gave more thought than any of his contemporaries, and continued to do so after he became a Roman Catholic, working on his *Grammar of Assent* for several decades. He saw the development of doctrine as taking its rise from individuals. 'It is individuals, and not the Holy See, that have taken the initiative, and given the lead to the Catholic mind, in theological inquiry' (Apo., p. 265). Newman had something fresh to say about the modes of individual apprehension of truths of faith. In his University Sermon on 'Implicit and Explicit Reason', he described the actual process as it is experienced. 'The mind ranges to and fro, and spreads out, and advances forward with a quickness which has become a proverb, and a subtlety and versatility which baffle investigation. It passes on from point to point, gaining one by some indication, another on a probability; then availing itself of an association; then falling back on some received law; next seizing on a testimony; then committing itself to some popular impression, or some inward instinct, or some obscure memory' (p. 257). He identified in all this the working of a growing certainty, which is 'moral' in both senses. That is, it is based on probability, and it has conscience to back it. 'Conscience is the essential principle and sanction of Religion in the mind' (University Sermon II, p. 18). Because it is doubly 'moral' it may exist, Newman

53 *Ibid.*, Proposition 52.
54 John Hey, *Lectures in Divinity* (Cambridge, 1796), pp. 390-5.

thinks, without being entirely conscious or explicit (University Sermon XIII, pp. 321-2), and for the same reason it may have a 'reality' and 'permanence' which makes it able to endure vicissitudes in understanding and experience (*ibid.*). Newman's own experience was of such a subtle, elusive but remorseless and continuous development of understanding.[55] There is an act of faith. 'While Opinion explicitly assents to the probability of a given proposition, Credence is an implicit assent to its truth' (*Grammar*, p. 46). But there most also be hard intellectual effort. 'We are so to understand what we do, so to master our thoughts and feelings, so to *recognize* what we believe, and how we believe, so to trace out our ideas and impressions, and to contemplate the issue of them, that we may be "ready always to give an answer to *every* man that asketh us an account of the hope that it is in us"' (University Sermon XIII, p. 253).

Newman is thinking here of 'reception' by individuals. He says as much in the same Sermon. There must be not only assent but development, an active working of the mind upon what is received (p. 313). We sometimes find a form of words 'out of shape and strange'. It may 'offend' the mind (pp. 270-1). It may strike us differently at different times (p. 271). But by patience and effort we acquire 'an active, ready, candid and docile mind, which can throw itself into what is said, neglect verbal difficulties, and pursue and carry out principles' (p. 275).[56] This is partly a matter of growing understanding enabling the mind to grasp at last what it could not at first. But it is also a process by which the same 'principles' are identified in different forms of words.

Newman sees this process in human minds as closely analogous with the collective activity of the reception process in the common mind. 'Doctrine may rather be said to use the minds of Christians, than to be used by them. Wonderful it is to see with what effort, hesitation, suspense, interruption - with how many swayings to the right and to the left - with how many reverses, yet with what certainty of advance, with what precision in its march, and with what ultimate completeness, it has been evolved; till the whole truth "self-balanced on its centre hung," part answerable to part, one, absolute, integral, indissoluble, while the world lasts!' (University Sermon XV, p. 317). 'At length a large fabric of divinity was reared, irregular in its structure, and diverse in its style, as beseemed the slow growth of centuries; nay, anomalous in its details, from the peculiarities of individuals, ... but still, on the whole, the development of an idea, and like itself, and unlike anything else, its most widely-separated parts having relations with

---

55 *From Bossuet to Newman*, p. 123.
56 Newman, *A Grammar of Assent*, ed. C.F. Harold (London, 1947), pp. xvii-iii.

each other and betokening a common origin' (p. 316).[57] The parallel here seems to lie in the variable and at times apparently underlying character of the development, within which, as Newman sees it, 'there is the gradual formation of a directing power out of a principle' (Dev. p. 361).

This 'naturalistic' description is an attempt on Newman's part to find a replacement for the formula of Vincent of Lérins, which he had come to find inadequate.[58] It depends for its 'evidential force' on the possibility of pointing to the continuity of what Newman calls an 'idea' in both the individual mind and the collective mind of the Church, so that the 'recognition' of reception is essentially the recognition that in a particular formula a known idea is being expressed. That needs to be set over against Rainy's notion of the 'office of the Church' (p. 129) in expressing the common mind of the faithful. Rainy says that the Church has, or may have, a common mind, and when she 'sets forth a collective utterance on doctrine, she is to be understood as setting forth in her own language what she judges with a common consent to be the teaching of Revelation' (p. 133). He, too, thinks that 'the Church embodies only on a larger scale the relation of the believing mind to the inspired Scriptures', although he confines the analogy more strictly to the Scriptural context than Newman does (p. 134). He develops rather more explicitly than Newman the point that there are different human aptitudes, so that some of the faithful contribute new inquiries, some cling to the past, some 'give voice to well-weighed, many-sided deliverances'; 'there are the question-raising minds ... the acquiescent minds' (p. 314). His point is that 'the Church of Christ is a community' (p. 135) and that it is as a community that it behaves in discharging its teaching office and in its 'care of doctrine' (pp. 140, 142).

By the time he published *Development*, Newman had begun to think that 'if the Christian doctrine, as originally taught, admits of true and important developments, ... this is a strong antecedent argument in favour of a provision in the dispensation, for putting a seal of authority upon those developments (pp. 117-9), first edition). That is in tune with his belief that something has now been completed which will last while the world lasts (*University Sermon*, XV, p. 317). This is further than he feels it necessary to go on the matter of evidence,[59] and it is worth underlining the contrast with the subtlety and complexity of the interplay he describes between the 'life' in the few words of the apostles, 'which shows itself in progress' (University Sermon, XIII, p. 318), and the 'life' which he sees as 'the mark

57 *From Bossuet to Newman*, p. 151, and cf. p. 99.
58 *Ibid.*, p. 66.
59 Newman, University Sermon, XIII, p. 260, 'Tillotson ... says: "Nothing ought to be received as a divine doctrine and revelation, without good evidence that it is so: that is, without some argument sufficient to satisfy a prudent and considerate man".'

of a true Church'[60] and the life of the individual human mind as it comes to grasp the faith. In the University Sermons he sets aside the question 'who is the legitimate framer and judge of these dogmatic inferences under the Gospel, or if there be any.' That seemed to him then to be 'not the point'. He wanted to concentrate not on 'whether the Church is infallible, or the individual, or the first ages, or none of these', 'but the theory of developments itself' (pp. 319-20). But in *Development* he was increasingly brought up against the problem of what Rainy calls 'the element of authoritative information' (p. 29), and in the *Apologia* and the *Grammar of Assent* he tries to deal with the notion of a final infallible authority in the Church which can set a seal on development and declare it perfected. He was particularly challenged to this view by his reading of William Chillingworth's *Religion of Protestants*. Chillingworth had argued that no believer could have an 'infallible faith' in the Church's teaching unless he believed the Church itself to be infallible; and since there is no 'infallible means to know that she is infallible', that is not possible (*Grammar*, p. 171). Newman tried various means of getting round this difficulty. He suggested that an infallible means need be no more than 'a means of coming at a fact without the chance of mistake'. It is, in other words, a secure means. He thought, too, that it is possible to believe in the infallible Church without that implying one's own infallibility (*Grammar*, pp. 171-2). He saw that a problem arises not only about the relation of a doctrine of infallible authority in the Church to the assent of the individual, but also about the relation of such a doctrine to the theology of reception. It is 'urged against the Catholic dogmas', he admits, that they do not have 'universal reception'. He argues that truth 'need not be universal, but it must of necessity be certain'. 'A truth or a fact may be certain, though it is not generally received', he repeats (*Grammar*, pp. 183-4).[61]

Much of what is problematic here arises because in Newman's scheme in his later life it was necessary to postulate not only the absoluteness of the deposit, the first gift of revelation to the Church, but also an absoluteness of the deposit, the first gift of revelation to the Church, but also an absoluteness at the other end of the story of development, in the form of a gift of infallibility to the Church in declaring truths of faith. Such truths Newman came to regard as requiring not a 'notional' but a 'real assent' (*Grammar*, p. 75).

---

[60] Newman, *Letters and Diaries*, XI, Letter of January 1846 to Wilberforce, p. 101, 'I believe I was the first writer who made life the mark of a true Church'.

[61] *Grammar of Assent*, pp. 167-70 on the indefectibility of certitude.

Common faith; common order

A number of underlying principles are clear in all this. First, unity in the faith has always been seen as a condition of membership of the Church, and of participation in its sacramental life. As Waterland puts it, 'Unity in fundamental articles of faith was always strictly insisted upon as one necessary condition of Church membership' (p. 75). Newman sees a further implication: the use of the 'test' of confession of the faith as a 'condition' of 'authority' in the Church.[62] Thus, if those in authority in a Church were to insist upon belief in some non-fundamental 'so far as to require us to deny any certain truth', or 'if any sinful terms whatever be imposed', they would cease to have any authority for the faithful. 'A breach of communion must follow of course ... and the imposers in such cases are the dividers', as Waterland puts it (p. 86). Waterland seems here to be bracketing faith with order, in his reference to 'sinful conditions'. Certainly he does so elsewhere, citing Hebrews 6.1 ff, with its references to both faith and sacramental life (p. 94). Wordsworth identifies 'the Church and the Ministry' as 'fundamental in a different sense' from the fundamentals of faith, as 'not so much concrete objects proposed for our acceptance, as necessary conditions of Christian life'. But the Church, it seems to him, 'is a society of believers, representing God to man', 'is presupposed' in the primitive Church's fundamentals of faith; 'the Ministry follows as the necessary instrument for keeping this life in its proper, regular and continuous course'.[63] Fundamentals of faith, the basis of right order, and the concomitant authority which is a necessary assurance of the validity of the sacraments in the community and of the rightness of decisions in matters of faith, are thus equally and inseparably concomitants of visible unity in the Church for the authors we have been citing. Hammond maintains that it is because of this interdependence of faith and order that the breach of order which is schism is 'contrary to the faith', even where it involves no heresy 'in respect of doctrinal points'. (On the other hand, where the conditions of communion with a Church 'contain in them any sin', it cannot be an act of schism to separate from it; for no Christian can be expected to make 'profession of an untruth' (*On Schism,* II.5-6, pp. 197-8, 204, 210). Thus, where there is already a disunity of faith or order, there is already schism, and the dissenter does not divide the Church, for its is already divided.)

Secondly, it follows that only within its proper order is the Church able to make decisions on matters of faith and order. The elements of that order are recognised by all our authors in different ways. Bullinger provides a convenient list in one of his Sermons. 'The Church doth not judge at her

---

62 Newman, *The Arians of the Fourth Century*, p. 149.
63 Wordsworth, *op. cit.*, pp. 10-11.

own pleasure, but after the sentence of the Holy Ghost, and according to the order and rule of the holy Scriptures'. There must also, he says, be 'order, moderation and charity'. When these are observed, and the Church 'giveth herself over to be guided by the Spirit, and examineth all her doings by the rule of the Word of God and of the twofold charity', only 'necessary things' are laid upon faithful Christians.[64]

There is a further lesson for unity. Grotius thought that no reason for discord can be so important that it would not be outweighed by a corresponding reason for concord. Christ acknowledges as his disciples only those who are peacemakers.[65] When Bullinger's 'order, moderation and charity are observed', or, as Hammond preferred to put it, 'those relations wherein each member of the whole Church of Christ is concerned one towards another', 'ecclesiastical unity' follows.[66] This 'external peace' or 'communion ecclesiastical'[67] must have visible form in the Church's order. Anglicans are heirs to the theology and practice of authority which has been discernible in the Church from the beginning, not only as catholic Christians and members of the Universal Church, but also, as Anglican history shows, by choice and by practice. 'There is such a thing as development in doctrine, and there can also be development in order and in the understanding of order 'within that heritage',[68] without in any way doing violence to the tradition. But such development must, if it is not to be divisive, waits upon reception. In matters of faith, a development which is imperfectly expressed, or not rightly balanced, can be put right. It is not so easy to put right an impatient move on a matter of order, especially one which touches the ordained ministry of a Communion, because division, or at the least serious damage to communion, must result if mutual recognition of ministry ceases to be possible.

That has, of course, occurred in the Anglican Communion as a result of the ordination of women, and especially of the consecration of women to the episcopate. Only if it is agreed that an unprecedented action which thus affects the common order is consonant with the apostolic faith can it be in the power of the Church to make the decision to act. (To decide to do so when that condition is fulfilled is another matter, because considerations other than that of sheer possibility then enter in: whether, for example, it is just; or whether it is appropriate in given local, cultural and contemporary circumstances.) The Church as a whole, that is, the universal Church,

---

64 Bullinger, Fifth *Decade*, Sermon i, p. 45.
65 Grotius, Introduction, 3, p. 76.
66 Schism, III.3, p. 212.
67 Schism, IX.1, p. 282.
68 *Proceedings* of the General Synod of the Church of England, 15th November, 1984, p. 1135.

patently has not yet made a decision about the ordination of women. The Anglican Communion has not done so either. Even in those provinces which have gone ahead there has been imperfect consensus at the time when local legislative provision was made, and there has had to be a system of safeguards for tender consciences. It has become painfully clear that a number of crucial issues are not yet resolved in Anglican thinking. What, for example, is the 'ecclesial status' of a province? It is usual to refer to the 'Churches' of the Anglican Communion rather than to 'the Anglican Church', and certainly a province is something more than a 'particular Church' in the sense in which we have been using that term.[69] On the other hand, in a single Communion independence must be balanced against interdependence, and rights against the imperative to act in common charity and with a catholic intention. We have been arguing that the question of order, as much as of the community of faith, is a responsibility of the universal Church in any matter which affects more than the local worshipping community.[70]

It is hard to say what constitute the non-negotiable fundamentals in matters of order. We can get a certain distance without dispute. There must be provision for a sacramental life, in which the validity of the sacraments is not in doubt. There must be pastoral leadership, not self-appointed, but recognised by those it serves as called and sent by the Holy Spirit and acting at the same time as the community's representative so that the community may be at one. There must be means of discipline. The ministry of the Word must be authoritative both within the existing community and in mission to those who are outside it. Most Christians would want to add that there must be oversight linking local worshipping communities in a visible whole in the larger Church. And many would now want to see that oversight as the ministry of unity in the universal Church. If that is right, we are agreed on what the fundamentals of order are, but not on the way in which they are to be made a concrete reality in the life of the future united Church. It may be that the stresses of the present Anglican crisis are serving a necessary purpose in crystallising the need to think the matter through ecumenically as well as domestically.

[69] See Lambeth, 1930, p. 155 and Lambeth, 1978, p. 83.
[70] If we want to say with the Niagara Report that continuity is carried on in the community of faith, we must regard this as precious.

Index

necessaries 120
necessary to salvation 9, 113, 99, 120
Netherlands 75
New Testament 19, 25, 26, 30, 66, 67, 70, 77
Newland 14, 89
Newman, John Henry 39, 73, 75, 118, 121, 122, 123, 132, 134, 136
Niagara Report 73
Nicaea 71
non necessaria 127
non-episcopal Churches 2, 74, 76
non-fundamentals 128
non-negotiable fundamentals 138
North Africa 71
notitia 9, 127
Nowell 9

obedience 19, 28, 97, 110, 124
office 23, 25, 27, 41, 66, 69, 77, 79, 110
officium 30
Old Testament 31, 37
one bishop, one diocese 33
one, holy, catholic and apostolic Church 76
ordaining 65
order 18, 20, 30, 73, 77, 78, 79, 87, 94, 117, 118, 136
orderliness 103
Ordinal 72, 101
ordinary 65
ordinary inherent jurisdiction 109, 110
ordination 24, 30, 34, 66, 67, 68, 70, 71, 73, 77, 81
ordination of a bishop 71
ordination of a priest 109
ordination of ministers 77
ordination of women 3, 137, 138 and Chapter 7 *passim*
ordinations 81
Orthodox Churches 2, 11, 36, 62, 72, 80
orthodox doctrine 34, 89
oversight 94, and see superintendence
Owen, John 21, 99

Pacem in terris 114
Palmer, William 122, 130, 131
papal decree 15
papal monarchy 43
Papal pronouncements 95
parish 62, 80
Parker, Matthew 72
Parliament 45, 111
particular churches 103

pastor 26, 29, 40
pastoral care 26, 77, 129
pastoral charge 79
pastoral epistles 25, 29
pastoral need 106
pastoral oversight 29
pastoral role 80
patriarchal Churches 46
Paul, Apostle 87
Paul the Deacon 30
peace 20, 28
penance 8, 106, 116
penitential canons 105
penitential system 98, 116
penitents 106
people of God 53, 81, 93, 97
permanence 133
perseverance 92
personal example 105
Petrus Cunaeus 127
Philippi 25
philosophy 88, 95
pluriformity 117
pontifex 25
Pope 44, 67
Pope Gregory the Great 27
post-Reformation 117
power 17, 23
power of the crucified 18
power to ordain 69, 70
practice 103
prayer 27, 77
Prayer Book 2, 101
preaching 8, 33, 109, 129
Predestination 117
presbyter-helpers 29
presbyterate 40, 67
presbyterial deputies 66
Presbyterians 78
presbyters 28
presbytery 37
presidency of the eucharistic community 80
presidents 29, 34, 37
priesthood 23, 24, 26, 30, 31, 62, 67, 69, 71, 72, 79, 82, 109
priesthood of all believers 23
priesthood of Christ 23
primacy 61, 62
primacy among equals 29
Primacy of Canterbury 61
primacy of jurisdiction 61
Primate 62, 94, 96